studysync®

Reading & Writing Companion

The Power of Communication

Why do words matter?

studysync

studysync.com

Send all inquiries to:
BookheadEd Learning, LLC
610 Daniel Young Drive
Sonoma, CA 95476

ISBN 978-1-94-469597-2

6 7 8 9 LMN 25 24 23 22 21

C

Student Guide

Getting Started

Welcome to the **StudySync Reading & Writing Companion!** In this book, you will find a collection of readings based on the theme of the unit you are studying. As you work through the readings, you will be asked to answer questions and perform a variety of tasks designed to help you closely analyze and understand each text selection. Read on for an explanation of each

Close Reading and Writing Routine

In each unit, you will read texts that share a common theme, despite their different genres, time periods, and authors. Each reading encourages a closer look through questions and a short writing assignment.

The Refusal
FICTION
Franz Kafka
1920

Introduction

studysync®

The Refusal

"In all important matters, however, the citizens can always count on a refusal."

Our little town does not lie on the frontier, nowhere near; it is so far from the frontier, in fact, that perhaps no one from our little town has ever been there; **desolate** highlands have to be crossed as well as wide fertile plains. To imagine even part of the road makes one tired, and more than part one just cannot imagine. There are also big towns on the road, each far larger than ours. Ten little towns like ours laid side by side, and ten more forced down from above, still would not produce one of those enormous, overcrowded towns. If one does not get lost on the way one is bound to lose oneself in these towns, and to avoid them is impossible on account of their size.

But what is even further from our town than the frontier, if such distances can be compared at all—it's like saying that a man of three hundred years is older than one of two hundred—what is even further than the frontier is the capital. Whereas we do get news of the frontier wars now and again, of the capital we learn next to nothing—we civilians that is, for of course the government officials have very good connections with the capital; they can get news from there in as little as three months, so they claim at least.

Now it is remarkable and I am continually being surprised at the way we in our town humbly submit to all orders issued in the capital. For centuries no political change has been brought about by the citizens themselves. In the capital great rulers have superseded each other—indeed, even dynasties have been deposed or annihilated, and new ones have started; in the past century even the capital itself was destroyed, a new one was founded far away from it, later on this too was destroyed and the old one rebuilt, yet none of this had any influence on our little town. Our officials have always remained at their posts; the highest officials came from the capital, the less high from other towns, and the lowest from among ourselves—that is how it has always been and it has suited us. The highest official is the chief tax-collector, he has the rank of colonel, and is known as such. The present one is an old man; I've known him for years, because he was already a colonel when I was a child.

Skill:
Textual Evidence

I think the narrator is talking about feeling distant from the power that rules their lives—the capital.

It says "we civilians" don't even get news of the capital; this is evidence of the narrator's distance from power.

Introduction

An Introduction to each text provides historical context for your reading as well as information about the author. You will also learn about the genre of the text and the year in which it was written.

Notes

Many times, while working through the activities after each text, you will be asked to **annotate** or **make annotations** about what you are reading. This means that you should highlight or underline words in the text and use the "Notes" column to make comments or jot down any questions you have. You may also want to note any unfamiliar vocabulary words here.

You will also see sample student annotations to go along with the Skill lesson for that text.

  Reading & Writing Companion

③ First Read

During your first reading of each selection, you should just try to get a general idea of the content and message of the reading. Don't worry if there are parts you don't understand or words that are unfamiliar to you. You'll have an opportunity later to dive deeper into the text.

④ Think Questions

These questions will ask you to start thinking critically about the text, asking specific questions about its purpose, and making connections to your prior knowledge and reading experiences. To answer these questions, you should go back to the text and draw upon specific evidence to support your responses. You will also begin to explore some of the more challenging vocabulary words in the selection.

⑤ Skills

Each Skill includes two parts: Checklist and Your Turn. In the Checklist, you will learn the process for analyzing the text. The model student annotations in the text provide examples of how you might make your own notes following the instructions in the Checklist. In the Your Turn, you will use those same instructions to practice the skill.

---

③ THE REFUSAL · First Read

Read "The Refusal." After you read, complete the Think Questions below.

④ ☁ THINK QUESTIONS

1. What can the reader infer about the tax-collector's power? Where does his power come from, and how is it expressed? Use evidence from the text to support your inferences.

2. What do you know about the relationship between the government, located in the faraway capital, and the small town? How do the villagers view the capital and the people who represent it? Cite evidence from the text to support your answer.

3. What role does the ceremony play in life in the small town? How do most townspeople feel about this custom? Support your answer with evidence from the text.

4. Use context clues to determine the meaning of **exceptional** as it is used in paragraph 5. Write your definition here and identify clues that helped you figure out its meaning.

5. Read the following dictionary entry:

   petition
   pe·ti·tion /pə'tiSH(ə)n/ *noun*

   1. A formal, written request to an authority
   2. A solemn appeal to a superior
   3. An application to a court for a judicial action

   Which definition most closely matches the meaning of **petition** as it is used in paragraph 5? Write the correct definition of *petition* here and explain how you figured out the meaning.

---

⑤ CHARACTER · Skill: Character

Use the Checklist to analyze Character in "The Refusal." Refer to the sample student annotations about Character in the text.

••• CHECKLIST FOR CHARACTER

In order to analyze how complex characters develop and interact in a text, note the following:

✓ the traits of complex characters in the text, such as a character that
  - has conflicting emotions and motivations
  - develops and changes over the course of a story or drama
  - advances the events of the plot
  - develops the central idea, or theme, through his or her actions

✓ the ways that characters respond, react, or change as the events of the plot unfold and how they interact with other characters in the story

✓ how the reactions and responses of complex characters help to advance the plot and develop the theme

To evaluate how complex characters develop and interact in a text, consider the following questions:

✓ Which characters in the text could be considered complex?

✓ Do the characters change as the plot unfolds? When do they begin to change? Which events cause them to change?

✓ How do any changes the characters undergo help to advance the plot and develop the theme?

---

⑤ ↻ YOUR TURN

1. The narrator's description of the colonel during the reception leads the reader to conclude that—

   ○ A. the colonel is considered to be an ordinary citizen.
   ○ B. the colonel is openly disrespected by the townspeople.
   ○ C. the colonel worries about losing his position as tax-collector.
   ○ D. the colonel inspires great fear among the townspeople.

2. The crowd's reaction to the colonel's refusal reveals that in this society—

   ○ A. the people feel dissatisfied with their government and plan to revolt.
   ○ B. the people are glad that nothing has happened to upset their traditions.
   ○ C. the people recognize that the colonel is a human being just as they are.
   ○ D. the people understand that the colonel is a powerless figurehead.

3. Which detail in the passage most clearly suggests that the colonel's character may be more complex than the townspeople realize?

   ○ A. He silently holds the two symbolic bamboo poles.
   ○ B. He breathes deeply and conspicuously, like a frog.
   ○ C. He drops the bamboo poles and sinks into a chair.
   ○ D. He reveals no emotion during the reception.

THE REFUSAL · Close Read ⑥

Reread "The Refusal." As you reread, complete the Skills Focus questions below. Then use your answers and annotations from the questions to help you complete the Write activity.

◎ SKILLS FOCUS

1. Paragraph 3 of "The Refusal" contains descriptions of the capital and the small town in which the story is set. Explain what you can infer about how the setting might affect the characters.

2. Analyze the townspeople's attitudes toward the soldiers and the colonel. Use textual evidence to explain what the different attitudes suggest about the characters' roles and interactions in the story.

3. In paragraph 7, the narrator reveals his feelings about the events in the town. Explain what you can infer about his character from this revelation and discuss how the details the narrator supplies help to advance the plot.

4. The young people in the final paragraph of the story are described as "discontent." Explain the likely source of their unhappiness and why this fact helps make them complex.

5. Discuss how the characters in "The Refusal" use language, or avoid using language, and how communication affects the events in the story.

✎ WRITE

LITERARY ANALYSIS: How does the author use the historical setting to create complex yet believable characters? Choose one or two characters to focus on and use evidence from the text to support your response.

⑦

12 Reading & Writing Companion

Roosevelts on the Radio

INFORMATIONAL TEXT

⑧

Introduction

A week after his inauguration, President Franklin Delano Roosevelt gave his first "fireside chat" to the nation over the radio. He, along with First Lady Eleanor, began an unprecedented series of radio addresses delivered directly to the American people. Their influence changed how Americans expect their politicians to communicate.

Ⓥ VOCABULARY

broadcasting
communicating to the public through radio or television

proficiency
expertise or skill

constituents
people who live in and vote in an area

infamy
the state of being well-known for disgraceful character or actions

⑧

---

⑥ Close Read & Skills Focus

After you have completed the First Read, you will be asked to go back and read the text more closely and critically. Before you begin your Close Read, you should read through the Skills Focus to get an idea of the concepts you will want to focus on during your second reading. You should work through the Skills Focus by making annotations, highlighting important concepts, and writing notes or questions in the "Notes" column. Depending on instructions from your teacher, you may need to respond online or use a separate piece of paper to start expanding on your thoughts and ideas.

⑦ Write

Your study of each selection will end with a writing assignment. For this assignment, you should use your notes, annotations, personal ideas, and answers to both the Think and Skills Focus questions. Be sure to read the prompt carefully and address each part of it in your writing.

⑧ English Language Learner

The English Language Learner texts focus on improving language proficiency. You will practice learning strategies and skills in individual and group activities to become better readers, writers, and speakers.

Extended Writing Project and Grammar

This is your opportunity to use genre characteristics and craft to compose meaningful, longer written works exploring the theme of each unit. You will draw information from your readings, research, and own life experiences to complete the assignment.

1 Writing Project

After you have read all of the unit text selections, you will move on to a writing project. Each project will guide you through the process of writing your essay. Student models will provide guidance and help you organize your thoughts. One unit ends with an **Extended Oral Project** which will give you an opportunity to develop your oral language and communication skills.

2 Writing Process Steps

There are four steps in the writing process: Plan, Draft, Revise, and Edit and Publish. During each step, you will form and shape your writing project, and each lesson's peer review will give you the chance to receive feedback from your peers and teacher.

3 Writing Skills

Each Skill lesson focuses on a specific strategy or technique that you will use during your writing project. Each lesson presents a process for applying the skill to your own work and gives you the opportunity to practice it to improve your writing.

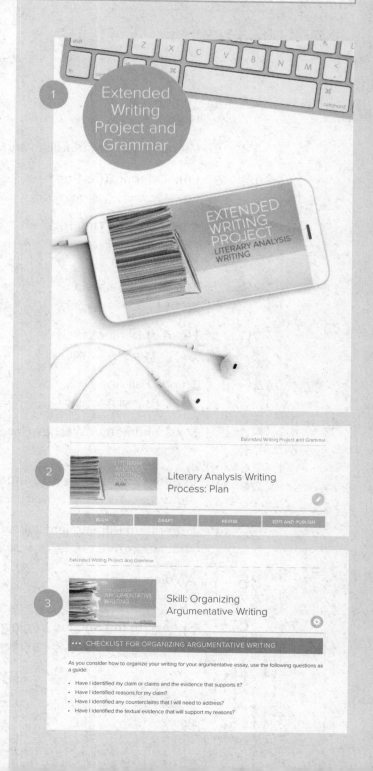

1 Extended Writing Project and Grammar

EXTENDED WRITING PROJECT LITERARY ANALYSIS WRITING

2 Literary Analysis Writing Process: Plan

| PLAN | DRAFT | REVISE | EDIT AND PUBLISH |

3 Skill: Organizing Argumentative Writing

CHECKLIST FOR ORGANIZING ARGUMENTATIVE WRITING

As you consider how to organize your writing for your argumentative essay, use the following questions as a guide:

- Have I identified my claim or claims and the evidence that supports it?
- Have I identified reasons for my claim?
- Have I identified any counterclaims that I will need to address?
- Have I identified the textual evidence that will support my reasons?

The Power of Communication

Why do words matter?

Genre Focus: FICTION

Texts

 Paired Readings

Extended Writing Project and Grammar

English Language Learner Resources

Unit 1: The Power of Communication
Why do words matter?

CHINUA ACHEBE

Chinua Achebe (1930–2013) is the author of the most widely read African novel of all time, *Things Fall Apart*. The work explores the intersection of traditional Igbo culture and Western colonialism, a reflection of Achebe's upbringing in an eastern Nigerian village at the center of a substantial Christian missionary effort. Achebe chose to write in English, offering a narrative of colonization that was shown, for the first time, from the perspective of the colonized.

HAYAN CHARARA

The son of Lebanese immigrants, Hayan Charara (b. 1972) grew up in Detroit, Michigan. His work explores themes of Arab American identity, family, and culture. He has published poetry collections, essays, and children's books, and edited *Inclined to Speak: An Anthology of Contemporary Arab American Poetry* (2008).

JOSEPH CONRAD

The Polish British writer Joseph Conrad (1857–1924) drew on his real-life experience as a merchant marine to write many of his stories, including the well-known and controversial book, *Heart of Darkness*. The novel offers a brutal portrayal of colonialism as its story follows a British riverboat captain's voyage up the Congo River in pursuit of ivory. Conrad chose to write primarily in English, his third language after Polish and French. In his autobiography, Conrad called English a language "of books read, of thoughts pursued, of remembered emotions—of my very dreams!"

PATRICK HENRY

Patrick Henry (1736–1799) was one of the Founding Fathers of the United States, the first and sixth governor of Virginia, and a key player in the American Revolution. He is perhaps best known for his address to the Virginia Legislature in 1775, where in an effort to incite opposition to the British government, he famously declared, "give me liberty or give me death!" Henry's manner of speech mirrored rhetorical gestures of evangelical sermons, a style he'd likely been exposed to as a child during the Great Awakening.

FRANZ KAFKA

The writing of Czech-born, German-speaking Franz Kafka (1883–1924) is so distinctive and well-known that his name is used as an adjective. The description of a situation as *Kafkaesque* means that it resembles the bizarre and disturbing predicaments inhabited by the characters in the author's stories. Ironically, Kafka's work received little recognition or publication in his lifetime, though he would later become regarded as a major figure of 20th-century Western literature.

MOHJA KAHF

Writer, activist, and professor Mohja Kahf (b. 1967) moved from her birthplace of Damascus, Syria, to the United States at an early age and grew up in the Midwest. Her work is shaped by both American and Arabic linguistic traditions and navigates questions of identity, diversity, and belonging. Such weight is balanced in Kahf's poems by the use of clear, accessible language paired with wit and humor.

MARTIN LUTHER KING JR.

Dr. Martin Luther King Jr. (1929–1968) was a Baptist minister and leader of the American civil rights movement. In 1963 King and other anti-segregation demonstrators were incarcerated in Birmingham, Alabama, when their campaign of nonviolent sit-ins, marches, and boycotts was met with violence from the local police. While in jail, King began writing his now famous "Letter from Birmingham Jail" in the margins of a newspaper. For his "steadfast commitment to achieving racial justice through nonviolent action," King was awarded the Nobel Peace Prize in 1964.

FRANCIS LA FLESCHE

Francis La Flesche (1857–1932) was a prominent Native American ethnologist who created an invaluable record of stories, songs, and rituals of the Omaha and Osage people. La Flesche was born on the Omaha Reservation and was sent by his parents to a mission school to learn English. His education and career were rooted in preserving the sophisticated and rich history of his ancestors. Much of the work was recorded on wax cylinders, the earliest commercial medium for converting and reproducing sound.

URSULA K. LE GUIN

Ursula K. Le Guin (1929–2018) was born and raised in Berkeley, California, but lived in Portland, Oregon, from 1958 until the end of her life. She was a prolific writer known for upending the conventions of the science fiction and fantasy genres, which, at the time she started writing in the 1960s, lacked any significant racial or gender diversity. She is best known for her fantasy series, Earthsea, and her anarchist utopian allegory, *The Dispossessed*.

JIMMY SANTIAGO BACA

Jimmy Santiago Baca (b. 1952), an American writer of Chicano and Apache descent, penned his first poems while serving a five-year prison sentence in his twenties. His poetry collection *Immigrants in Our Own Land* (1979) draws on his experience of incarceration and, like much of his work, deftly addresses themes of social justice, addiction, and community in the barrios of the American Southwest.

PAT MORA

Pat Mora (b. 1942) is a Mexican American poet, writer, and popular national speaker. Originally from El Paso, Texas, Mora gives voice to those navigating a divided identity in the context of the border region between the United States and Mexico. Her poetry employs both English and Spanish words, addressing cultural intersection not only in theme, but through language itself.

The Refusal

FICTION
Franz Kafka
1920

Introduction

Born in a Jewish ghetto in Prague, Franz Kafka (1883–1924) allegedly burned up to 90 percent of his own work during his lifetime. Luckily, a few important pieces survived—enough to shape his legacy as one of the most influential 20th-century writers, whose depictions of bizarre and sinister events in a society under bureaucratic control coined the term 'Kafkaesque'. Written in 1920, "The Refusal" depicts a ritual ceremony in a small town controlled by a government in a faraway capital. In times of need, residents of the town appeal to the tax-collector, the town's highest ranking government official, for help. The text's themes of oppression and authoritarianism would have resonated strongly with a readership that had just endured World War I and was on the brink of another global conflict.

"In all important matters, however, the citizens can always count on a refusal."

NOTES

1   Our little town does not lie on the frontier, nowhere near; it is so far from the frontier, in fact, that perhaps no one from our little town has ever been there; **desolate** highlands have to be crossed as well as wide fertile plains. To imagine even part of the road makes one tired, and more than part one just cannot imagine. There are also big towns on the road, each far larger than ours. Ten little towns like ours laid side by side, and ten more forced down from above, still would not produce one of those enormous, overcrowded towns. If one does not get lost on the way one is bound to lose oneself in these towns, and to avoid them is impossible on account of their size.

2   But what is even further from our town than the frontier, if such distances can be compared at all—it's like saying that a man of three hundred years is older than one of two hundred—what is even further than the frontier is the capital. Whereas we do get news of the frontier wars now and again, of the capital we learn next to nothing—we civilians that is, for of course the government officials have very good connections with the capital; they can get news from there in as little as three months, so they claim at least.

3   Now it is remarkable and I am continually being surprised at the way we in our town humbly submit to all orders issued in the capital. For centuries no political change has been brought about by the citizens themselves. In the capital great rulers have superseded each other—indeed, even dynasties have been deposed or annihilated, and new ones have started; in the past century even the capital itself was destroyed, a new one was founded far away from it, later on this too was destroyed and the old one rebuilt, yet none of this had any influence on our little town. Our officials have always remained at their posts; the highest officials came from the capital, the less high from other towns, and the lowest from among ourselves—that is how it has always been and it has suited us. The highest official is the chief tax-collector, he has the rank of colonel, and is known as such. The present one is an old man; I've known him for years, because he was already a colonel when I was a child. At first he rose very fast in his career, but then he seems to have advanced no further; actually, for our little town his rank is good enough, a higher rank would be out of place. When I try to recall him I see him sitting on the veranda of his house in the Market Square, leaning back, pipe in mouth. Above him

Skill:
Textual Evidence

I think the narrator is talking about feeling distant from the power that rules their lives— the capital.

It says "we civilians" don't even get news of the capital; this is evidence of the narrator's distance from power.

**Skill:
Character**

On one hand the colonel is the most powerful man in town, but on the other hand it seems like he didn't try to be so powerful; he just went along with becoming the top official just like the rest of the town did. What motivates him?

from the roof flutters the imperial flag; on the sides of the veranda, which is so big that minor military maneuvers are sometimes held there, washing hangs out to dry. His grandchildren, in beautiful silk clothes, play around him; they are not allowed down in the Market Square, the children there are considered unworthy of them, but the grandchildren are attracted by the square, so they thrust their heads between the posts of the banister and when the children below begin to quarrel they join the quarrel from above.

4   This colonel, then, commands the town. I don't think he has ever produced a document entitling him to this position; very likely he does not possess such a thing. Maybe he really is chief tax-collector. But is that all? Does that entitle him to rule over all the other departments in the administration as well? True, his office is very important for the government, but for the citizens it is hardly the most important. One is almost under the impression that the people here say: "Now that you've taken all we possess, please take us as well." In reality, of course, it was not he who seized the power, nor is he a tyrant. It has just come about over the years that the chief tax-collector is automatically the top official, and the colonel accepts the tradition just as we do.

5   Yet while he lives among us without laying too much stress on his official position, he is something quite different from the ordinary citizen. When a delegation comes to him with a request, he stands there like the wall of the world. Behind him is nothingness, one imagines hearing voices whispering in the background, but this is probably a delusion; after all, he represents the end of all things, at least for us. At these receptions he really was worth seeing. Once as a child I was present when a delegation of citizens arrived to ask him for a government subsidy because the poorest quarter of the town had been burned to the ground. My father the blacksmith, a man well respected in the community, was a member of the delegation and had taken me along. There's nothing exceptional about this, everyone rushes to spectacles of this kind, one can hardly distinguish the actual delegation from the crowd. Since these receptions usually take place on the veranda, there are even people who climb up by ladder from the Market Square and take part in the goings-on from over the bannister. On this occasion about a quarter of the veranda had been reserved for the colonel, the crowd kept filling the rest of it. A few soldiers kept watch, some of them standing round him in a semicircle. Actually a single soldier would have been quite enough, such is our fear of them. I don't know exactly where these soldiers come from, in any case from a long way off, they all look very much alike, they wouldn't even need a uniform. They are small, not strong but agile people, the most striking thing about them is the prominence of their teeth which almost overcrowd their mouths, and a certain restless twitching of their small narrow eyes. This makes them the terror of the children, but also their delight, for again and again the children long to be frightened by these teeth, these eyes, so as to be able to run away in horror. Even grownups probably never quite lose this

Reading & Writing Companion

Skill:
Text-Dependent
Responses

childish terror, at least it continues to have an effect. There are, of course, other factors contributing to it. The soldiers speak a dialect utterly incomprehensible to us, and they can hardly get used to ours—all of which produces a certain shut-off, unapproachable quality corresponding, as it happens, to their character, for they are silent, serious, and **rigid.** They don't actually do anything evil, and yet they are almost unbearable in an evil sense. A soldier, for example, enters a shop, buys some trifling object, and stays there leaning against the counter; he listens to the conversations, probably does not understand them, and yet gives the impression of understanding; he himself does not say a word, just stares blankly at the speaker, then back at the listeners, all the while keeping his hand on the hilt of the long knife in his belt. This is revolting, one loses the desire to talk, the customers start leaving the shop, and only when it is quite empty does the soldier also leave. Thus wherever the soldiers appear, our lively people grow silent. That's what happened this time, too. As on all solemn occasions the colonel stood upright, holding in front of him two poles of bamboo in his outstretched hands. This is an ancient custom implying more or less that he supports the law, and the law supports him. Now everyone knows, of course, what to expect up on the veranda, and yet each time people take fright all over again. On this occasion, too, the man chosen to speak could not begin, he was already standing opposite the colonel when his courage failed him and, muttering a few excuses, he pushed his way back into the crowd. No other suitable person willing to speak could be found, albeit several unsuitable ones offered themselves; a great commotion ensued and messengers went in search of various citizens who were well-known speakers. During all this time the colonel stood there motionless, only his chest moving visibly up and down to his breathing. Not that he breathed with difficulty, it was just that he breathed so conspicuously, much as frogs breathe—except that with them it is normal, while here it was **exceptional.** I squeezed myself through the grownups and watched him through a gap between two soldiers, until one of them kicked me away with his knee. Meanwhile the man originally chosen to speak had regained his composure and, firmly held up by two fellow citizens, was delivering his address. It was touching to see him smile throughout this solemn speech describing a grievous misfortune—a most humble smile which strove in vain to elicit some slight reaction on the colonel's face. Finally he formulated the request—I think he was only asking for a year's tax exemption, but possibly also for timber from the imperial forests at a reduced price. Then he bowed low, as did everyone else except the colonel, the soldiers, and a number of officials in the background. To the child it seemed ridiculous that the people on the ladders should climb down a few rungs so as not to be seen during the significant pause and now and again peer inquisitively over the floor of the veranda. After this had lasted quite a while an official, a little man, stepped up to the colonel and tried to reach the latter's height by standing on his toes. The colonel, still motionless save for his deep breathing, whispered something in his ear, whereupon the little man clapped

The townspeople are terrified of the soldiers, who come from far away and speak an unfamiliar language.

his hands and everyone rose. "The **petition** has been refused," he announced. "You may go." An undeniable sense of relief passed through the crowd, everyone surged out, hardly a soul paying any special attention to the colonel, who, as it were, had turned once more into a human being like the rest of us. I still caught one last glimpse of him as he wearily let go of the poles, which fell to the ground, then sank into an armchair produced by some officials, and promptly put his pipe in his mouth.

6   This whole occurrence is not isolated, it's in the general run of things. Indeed, it does happen now and again that minor petitions are granted, but then it invariably looks as though the colonel had done it as a powerful private person on his own responsibility, and it had to be kept all but a secret from the government—not **explicitly** of course, but that is what it feels like. No doubt in our little town the colonel's eyes, so far as we know, are also the eyes of the government, and yet there is a difference which it is impossible to comprehend completely.

7   In all important matters, however, the citizens can always count on a refusal. And now the strange fact is that without this refusal one simply cannot get along, yet at the same time these official occasions designed to receive the refusal are by no means a formality. Time after time one goes there full of expectation and in all seriousness and then one returns, if not exactly strengthened or happy, nevertheless not disappointed or tired. About these things I do not have to ask the opinion of anyone else, I feel them in myself, as everyone does; nor do I have any great desire to find out how these things are connected.

8   As a matter of fact, there is, so far as my observations go, a certain age group that is not content—these are the young people roughly between seventeen and twenty. Quite young fellows, in fact, who are utterly incapable of foreseeing the consequences of even the least significant, far less a revolutionary, idea. And it is among just them that discontent creeps in.

Skill:
Text-Dependent Responses

Use the Checklist to analyze Text-Dependent Responses in "The Refusal." Refer to the sample student annotations about Text-Dependent Responses in the text.

••• CHECKLIST FOR TEXT-DEPENDENT RESPONSES

In order to cite strong and thorough textual evidence that supports an analysis, consider the following:

✓ Inferences are sound and logical assumptions about information in a text that is not explicitly or directly stated by the author.

- Read closely and critically and consider why an author gives or excludes particular details and information.

- Apply your own knowledge, experiences, and observations along with textual evidence to help you figure out what the author does not state directly.

- Cite several pieces of textual evidence that offer the strongest, most thorough and comprehensive support for your analysis.

✓ To make a point, authors often provide explicit evidence of a character's feelings or motivations, or the reasons behind an historical event in a nonfiction text.

- Explicit evidence is stated directly in the text and must be cited accurately to support a text-dependent response or analysis.

To cite strong and thorough textual evidence that supports an analysis, consider the following questions:

✓ Can the question be answered by citing explicit evidence in the text, such as a direct cause-and-effect relationship?

✓ If I infer things in the text that the author does not state directly, what evidence from the text, along with my own experiences and knowledge, can I use to support my analysis?

✓ Have I used textual evidence that offers the strongest support for my analysis? How do I know?

Skill:
Text-Dependent Responses

Reread paragraph 3 of "The Refusal." Then, using the Checklist on the previous page, answer the multiple-choice questions below.

YOUR TURN

1. In paragraph 3, the narrator reveals that the tax-collector's grandchildren "are not allowed down in the Market Square." Which commentary best responds to this textual evidence?

   ○ A The tax-collector's grandchildren are special and considered far above the status of the townspeople's children.

   ○ B The tax-collector's grandchildren think they are better than the townspeople's children and refuse to play with them.

   ○ C The tax-collector's grandchildren adore their grandfather but look down on the townspeople's children.

   ○ D The tax-collector's grandchildren are spoiled by the time and attention lavished on them and do not like to play with other children.

2. Which quotation from the text best supports a reader's response that claims "although the villagers have no power of their own, events in the faraway capital have little effect on them"?

   ○ A "Now it is remarkable and I am continually being surprised at the way we in our town humbly submit to all orders issued in the capital."

   ○ B "For centuries no political change has been brought about by the citizens themselves."

   ○ C "In the capital great rulers have superseded each other—indeed, even dynasties have been deposed or annihilated, and new ones have started . . ."

   ○ D ". . . in the past century even the capital itself was destroyed, a new one was founded far away from it, later on this too was destroyed and the old one rebuilt, yet none of this had any influence on our little town."

First Read

Read "The Refusal." After you read, complete the Think Questions below.

☁ THINK QUESTIONS

1. What can the reader infer about the tax-collector's power? Where does his power come from, and how is it expressed? Use evidence from the text to support your inferences.

2. What do you know about the relationship between the government, located in the faraway capital, and the small town? How do the villagers view the capital and the people who represent it? Cite evidence from the text to support your answer.

3. What role does the ceremony play in life in the small town? How do most townspeople feel about this custom? Support your answer with evidence from the text.

4. Use context clues to determine the meaning of **exceptional** as it is used in paragraph 5. Write your definition here and identify clues that helped you figure out its meaning.

5. Read the following dictionary entry:

petition

pe•ti•tion /pə'tiSH(ə)n/ *noun*

1. A formal, written request to an authority
2. A solemn appeal to a superior
3. An application to a court for a judicial action

Which definition most closely matches the meaning of **petition** as it is used in paragraph 5? Write the correct definition of *petition* here and explain how you figured out the meaning.

Please note that excerpts and passages in the StudySync® library and this workbook are intended as touchstones to generate interest in an author's work. The excerpts and passages do not substitute for the reading of entire texts, and StudySync® strongly recommends that students seek out and purchase the whole literary or informational work in order to experience it as the author intended. Links to online resellers are available in our digital library. In addition, complete works may be ordered through an authorized reseller by filling out and returning to StudySync® the order form enclosed in this workbook.

Reading & Writing Companion   7

Skill:
Textual Evidence

Use the Checklist to analyze Textual Evidence in "The Refusal." Refer to the sample student annotations about Textual Evidence in the text.

••• CHECKLIST FOR TEXTUAL EVIDENCE

In order to support an analysis by citing evidence that is explicitly stated in the text, do the following:

- ✓ Read the text closely and critically.

- ✓ Identify what the text says explicitly.

- ✓ Find the most relevant textual evidence that supports your analysis.

- ✓ Consider why an author explicitly states specific details and information.

- ✓ Cite the specific words, phrases, sentences, or paragraphs from the text that support your analysis.

In order to interpret implicit meanings in a text by making inferences, do the following:

- ✓ Combine information directly stated in the text with your own knowledge, experiences, and observations.

- ✓ Cite the specific words, phrases, sentences, or paragraphs from the text that lead to and support this inference.

In order to cite textual evidence to support an analysis of what the text says explicitly as well as inferences drawn from the text, consider the following questions:

- ✓ Have I read the text closely and critically?

- ✓ What inferences am I making about the text?

- ✓ What textual evidence am I using to support these inferences?

- ✓ Am I quoting the evidence from the text correctly?

- ✓ Does my textual evidence logically relate to my analysis or the inference I am making?

Copyright © BookheadEd Learning, LLC

Skill:
Textual Evidence

Reread paragraph 5 of "The Refusal." Then, using the Checklist on the previous page, answer the multiple-choice questions below.

🔁 YOUR TURN

1. Which of the following statements from the text provides the best evidence for the inference that the soldiers are seen as beastlike and inhuman?

   ○ A. "Thus wherever the soldiers appear, our lively people grow silent."
   ○ B. "This is revolting, one loses the desire to talk, the customers start leaving the shop, and only when it is quite empty does the soldier also leave."
   ○ C. "A soldier, for example, . . . listens to the conversations, probably does not understand them, and yet gives the impression of understanding. . . ."
   ○ D. "They are small, not strong but agile people, the most striking thing about them is the prominence of their teeth which almost overcrowd their mouths, and a certain restless twitching of their small narrow eyes."

2. Which of the following facts provides the best textual evidence for the inference that the people of the village do not hope for change?

   ○ A. They find it very difficult to request things from the colonel.
   ○ B. Even the colonel sinks into his chair after the ceremony.
   ○ C. They are comforted by a predictable refusal.
   ○ D. Even very reasonable requests are always refused.

Skill:
Character

Use the Checklist to analyze Character in "The Refusal." Refer to the sample student annotations about Character in the text.

••• CHECKLIST FOR CHARACTER

In order to analyze how complex characters develop and interact in a text, note the following:

✓ the traits of complex characters in the text, such as a character that

- has conflicting emotions and motivations
- develops and changes over the course of a story or drama
- advances the events of the plot
- develops the central idea, or theme, through his or her actions

✓ the ways that characters respond, react, or change as the events of the plot unfold and how they interact with other characters in the story

✓ how the reactions and responses of complex characters help to advance the plot and develop the theme

To evaluate how complex characters develop and interact in a text, consider the following questions:

✓ Which characters in the text could be considered complex?

✓ Do the characters change as the plot unfolds? When do they begin to change? Which events cause them to change?

✓ How do any changes the characters undergo help to advance the plot and develop the theme?

Skill:
Character

Reread paragraph 5 of "The Refusal." Then, using the Checklist on the previous page, answer the multiple-choice questions below.

⟳ YOUR TURN

1. The narrator's description of the colonel during the reception leads the reader to conclude that—

   ○ A. the colonel is considered to be an ordinary citizen.
   ○ B. the colonel is openly disrespected by the townspeople.
   ○ C. the colonel worries about losing his position as tax-collector.
   ○ D. the colonel inspires great fear among the townspeople.

2. The crowd's reaction to the colonel's refusal reveals that in this society—

   ○ A. the people feel dissatisfied with their government and plan to revolt.
   ○ B. the people are glad that nothing has happened to upset their traditions.
   ○ C. the people recognize that the colonel is a human being just as they are.
   ○ D. the people understand that the colonel is a powerless figurehead.

3. Which detail in the passage most clearly suggests that the colonel's character may be more complex than the townspeople realize?

   ○ A. He silently holds the two symbolic bamboo poles.
   ○ B. He breathes deeply and conspicuously, like a frog.
   ○ C. He drops the bamboo poles and sinks into a chair.
   ○ D. He reveals no emotion during the reception.

Please note that excerpts and passages in the StudySync® library and this workbook are intended as touchstones to generate interest in an author's work. The excerpts and passages do not substitute for the reading of entire texts, and StudySync® strongly recommends that students seek out and purchase the whole literary or informational work in order to experience it as the author intended. Links to online resellers are available in our digital library. In addition, complete works may be ordered through an authorized reseller by filling out and returning to StudySync® the order form enclosed in this workbook.

Reading & Writing
Companion

11

Close Read

Reread "The Refusal." As you reread, complete the Skills Focus questions below. Then use your answers and annotations from the questions to help you complete the Write activity.

◎ SKILLS FOCUS

1. Paragraph 3 of "The Refusal" contains descriptions of the capital and the small town in which the story is set. Explain what you can infer about how the setting might affect the characters.

2. Analyze the townspeople's attitudes toward the soldiers and the colonel. Use textual evidence to explain what the different attitudes suggest about the characters' roles and interactions in the story.

3. In paragraph 7, the narrator reveals his feelings about the events in the town. Explain what you can infer about his character from this revelation and discuss how the details the narrator supplies help to advance the plot.

4. The young people in the final paragraph of the story are described as "discontent." Explain the likely source of their unhappiness and why this fact helps make them complex.

5. Discuss how the characters in "The Refusal" use language, or avoid using language, and how communication affects the events in the story.

✏ WRITE

LITERARY ANALYSIS: How does the author use the historical setting to create complex yet believable characters? Choose one or two characters to focus on and use evidence from the text to support your response.

Copyright © BookheadEd Learning, LLC

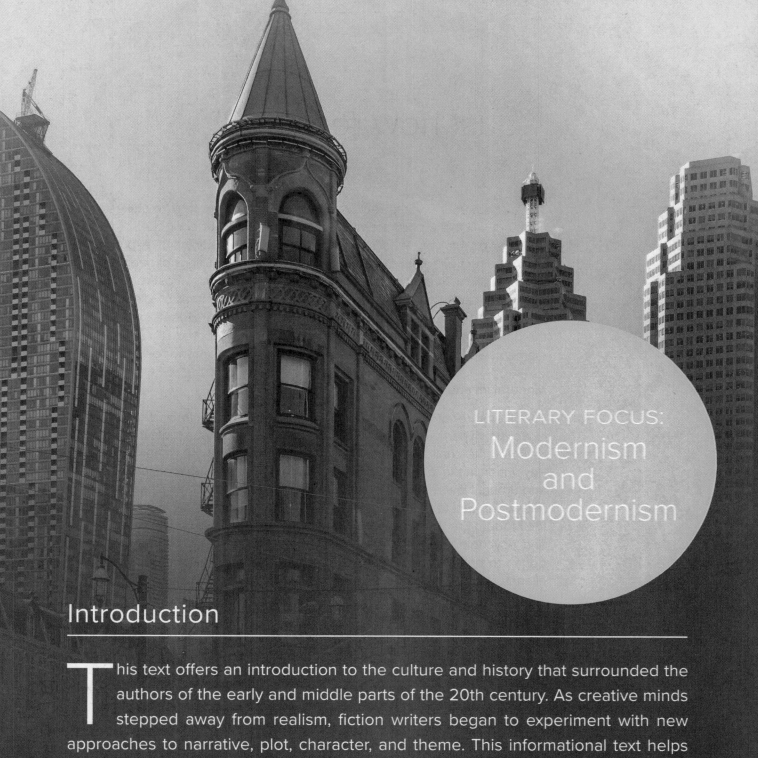

Introduction

This text offers an introduction to the culture and history that surrounded the authors of the early and middle parts of the 20th century. As creative minds stepped away from realism, fiction writers began to experiment with new approaches to narrative, plot, character, and theme. This informational text helps audiences understand how art and works of literature written in different periods of the 20th century compare. What makes *Things Fall Apart* so different from *Heart of Darkness*? This overview gives insight into the new ideas and modern interests that informed the writers who lived through World War I and World War II to see a new world before their eyes and across the page.

"Just how real is it?"

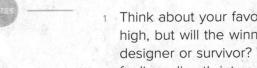

1   Think about your favorite reality show. Just how real is it? The stakes seem high, but will the winner actually be America's top model or chef or fashion designer or survivor? What's really going on when participants express their feelings directly into a camera? Surely they know that millions of people will be watching them. Even though the word *reality* is in the title, most reality shows are in fact carefully constructed narratives pieced together by directors and producers. The dramatic confrontations, the way viewers identify with or vilify the participants, the self-aware finales, and the fragmented storylines are all elements with roots in literary periods known as modernism and postmodernism.

Modernism and the Modern World

2   The literature of the nineteenth century was characterized by realism. Novelists, in particular, created stories with characters and plots that faithfully reflected the challenges and issues of their time. With the Second Industrial Revolution in the late 1800s, daily life became more fast-paced, mechanized, and urban. New research and analysis by scientists such as Charles Darwin and Albert Einstein and the psychoanalyst Sigmund Freud helped usher in the Modern Era. This era was a time of science and progress, rational thought and psychology. After World War I (1914–1918), traditional class structures began to break down in Europe and the United States. Modern writers felt alienated from the stable, pre-war world they had previously known.

3   As a result, many rejected realism, the practice of representing or depicting people, places, and situations as close to how they look in real life as possible. Instead, their works explored the subjective **interiority** of a narrator's inner life and the **fragmentation** of time. Virginia Woolf's *Mrs. Dalloway* and James Joyce's *Ulysses* are classic examples of modernism. The novels lack linear plot, chronology, and a reliable narrator. Instead, writers used **stream of consciousness** to move the narrative forward. With stream of consciousness, writers endeavor to mimic natural human patterns of thought which can shift quickly from one thought or observation to the next in a seemingly random or chaotic manner. This technique makes modernist novels highly stylized, reflecting the author's unique voice. Much like the literature, modernist art also rejected realism and hinted at characters' inner worlds, as in Picasso's painting *Girl Before A Mirror*, whose colorful distortions depict a girl looking inward as she stands in front of a mirror, perhaps self-consciously.

Copyright © Bookheaded Learning, LLC

Girl Before A Mirror by Pablo Picasso (1932)

Postmodernism and the Post-War World

4   With the end of World War II in 1945 came the collapse of European colonialism, the emergence of new nations, and the rise of multicultural voices by authors with new stories to tell and new ways to tell them. Postmodern literature regularly features everyday language, narrative fragmentation, and **experimentalism**.

5   Postmodern texts often have unexpected and challenging structures. Other times, authors use conventional structures, but subvert an existing story by modifying its genre or form, or updating it in some other way. In some examples of postmodernist literature, each chapter in a novel might tell the story from a different character's experience, or the story might start in the middle of the narrative and never reach a satisfying conclusion, as in Julio Cortazar's story "House Taken Over." Like the participants in a reality show, postmodern authors and their narrators are ironic; they understand that they—and the readers—are "in on" the act of storytelling. They reveal their self-awareness through quoting, referring to, or **parodying** other texts. For example, Seth Grahame-Smith updated Jane Austen's *Pride and Prejudice* by adding zombies, mixing two genres and putting his own spin on the classic and well-known novel. Unlike modernist writers, postmodernist writers focus on **exteriority**. They are frequently more interested in the external world and its social and cultural constructs than in a character's inner thoughts and feelings. They often convey the complexity of the postmodern world by using **multiplication** or several narrators. Each narrator has his or her own unique and often conflicting perspectives. Sometimes a postmodern author inserts himself or herself—or a character that is very close to him or her—into the narrative. In postmodern art such as Escher's *Convex and Concave*, the artist

Please note that excerpts and passages in the StudySync® library and this workbook are intended as touchstones to generate interest in an author's work. The excerpts and passages do not substitute for the reading of entire texts, and StudySync® strongly recommends that students seek out and purchase the whole literary or informational work in order to experience it as the author intended. Links to online resellers are available in our digital library. In addition, complete works may be ordered through an authorized reseller by filling out and returning to StudySync® the order form enclosed in this workbook.

Reading & Writing Companion

15

NOTES

plays with perspective much like postmodern writers, but in this case by carefully constructing vanishing points so that one could see a different exterior world with each turn of the piece.

Convex and Concave by M.C. Escher, 1955

Major Concepts

	Modernist Literature	Postmodernist Literature
Point of View	The focus is on the author's subjective style and point of view.	The focus is on the reader's experience of reading the text and the author's awareness of that experience.
Character	The author uses interiority, stream of consciousness, and inner monologue to explore the narrator's or character's psychology.	The author may concentrate on exteriority, often through a third-person omniscient narrator who focuses on the social or physical world.
Narrative Coherence	The author may employ unreliable narrators, nonlinear time sequences, and complicated language.	The author creates multiplication of meaning through multiple narrators with multiple perspectives on the same issue.
Themes	Themes often include alienation, escapism, and unstable or fragmented identity. Franz Kafka's story "The Refusal" is a classic example of the modernist themes of alienation and uncertain identity.	Themes often reflect collective voices and multicultural experiences.

6

Style and Form

7

	Modernist Literature	Postmodernist Literature
Language	The author often uses uncommon, sophisticated, or made-up language to express a subjective experience or point of view.	The author uses clear, everyday language to engage the audience and offset the often complicated narrative structure.
Narration	Stories are often presented in a subjective, often fragmented or nonlinear way. As an example, consider the complicated logic of Marlow, the narrator of Joseph Conrad's *Heart of Darkness*.	Stories are often presented in a fragmented or nonlinear way by an ironic narrator or multiple narrators. Chinua Achebe explores the opposing but equally sympathetic perspectives of Okonkwo and his father in *Things Fall Apart*.
Genre	Modernist writers experiment with storytelling elements, such as linear plot structures and character, but generally do not break from established genres. In modernism, literature is still considered an art form.	Postmodernist writers show self-awareness of genre forms by quoting or parodying other texts. Postmodern texts mix and give equal weight to "high culture" and popular culture.

8   Though different in style and form, modernist and postmodernist literature reflect a complicated and ever-changing reality. Modernists examined the world through a deeply subjective lens, while postmodernists tend to be more interested in a multiplicity of voices and experiences. Postmodernist texts continue to challenge readers and evolve into new forms today. Where do you notice the influence of modernism and postmodernism in popular culture?

Literary Focus

Read "Literary Focus: Modernism and Postmodernism." After you read, complete the Think Questions below.

☁ THINK QUESTIONS

1. What are the major differences between modernist and postmodernist works in terms of how authors craft their characters? Cite evidence from the text that backs up your explanations.

2. What effect did both world wars have on the literature that followed? Explain, using evidence from the text to support your inferences.

3. Think of two or three texts you have read in school that were written in the 20th century. Write down their titles and explain, based on the information here, whether you think they are modernist or postmodernist works. Use evidence from this text to support your assertions.

4. The word **fragmentation** stems from the Latin *frangere*, meaning "to break or shatter." With this information in mind, determine the meaning of *fragmentation* as it is used within the context of an informational text about literature. Cite any words or phrases from the text that were helpful in coming to your conclusion.

5. Use context clues to determine the meaning of the word **exteriority**. Write your definition here, along with the words or phrases that were most helpful in determining the word's meaning. Finally, check a dictionary to confirm your understanding.

I Am Offering This Poem

POETRY
Jimmy Santiago Baca
1979

Introduction

The tender words of this poem give little hint of the poet's rough life, but Jimmy Santiago Baca (b. 1952) says he doesn't know if he'd be alive today if he hadn't found poetry. Born in New Mexico of Apache and Chicano descent, Baca was abandoned by his parents as a toddler and later sent to an orphanage, which he fled at the age of 13 to live on the streets. By the time he was 21, Baca was in jail for drugs. It was there he began to turn his life around, learning to read and write poetry while serving a six-and-a-half-year prison sentence. Since his release, he has dedicated his life to teaching others the saving grace of writing.

"I am offering this poem to you . . ."

1   I am offering this poem to you,
2   since I have nothing else to give.
3   Keep it like a warm coat
4   when winter comes to cover you,
5   or like a pair of thick socks
6   the cold cannot bite through,

7   I love you,

8   I have nothing else to give you,
9   so it is a pot full of yellow corn
10   to warm your belly in winter,
11   it is a scarf for your head, to wear
12   over your hair, to tie up around your face,

13   I love you,

14   Keep it, treasure this as you would
15   if you were lost, needing **direction**,
16   in the wilderness life becomes when **mature**;
17   and in the corner of your drawer,
18   tucked away like a cabin or **hogan**
19   in **dense** trees, come knocking,
20   and I will answer, give you directions,
21   and let you warm yourself by this fire,
22   rest by this fire, and make you feel safe

23   I love you,

24   It's all I have to give,
25   and all anyone needs to live,
26   and to go on living inside,
27   when the world outside

28 no longer cares if you live or die;
29 remember,
30 I love you

By Jimmy Santiago Baca, from IMMIGRANTS IN OUR OWN LAND, copyright
©1979 by Jimmy Santiago Baca. Reprinted by permission of New Directions
Publishing Corp.

✏ WRITE

PERSONAL RESPONSE: Often, people give gifts that are tangible or material. However, in this poem, the gift is one of words. How does what you read influence your opinion on what makes a good gift? Cite evidence from the poem as well as from your personal experience to support your opinion.

Please note that excerpts and passages in the StudySync® library and this workbook are intended as touchstones to generate interest in an author's work. The excerpts and passages do not substitute for the reading of entire texts, and StudySync® strongly recommends that students seek out and purchase the whole literary or informational work in order to experience it as the author intended. Links to online resellers are available in our digital library. In addition, complete works may be ordered through an authorized reseller by filling out and returning to StudySync® the order form enclosed in this workbook.

Reading & Writing
Companion

21

She Unnames Them

FICTION
Ursula K. Le Guin
1985

Introduction

Ursula K. Le Guin (1929–2018) was a beloved and influential science-fiction author. Deeply engaged with issues of feminism and the environment, she won the Hugo and Nebula awards for her novel *The Left Hand of Darkness*. Le Guin's short story "She Unnames Them" reimagines a foundational passage from the Book of Genesis in which Adam names the different animals he encounters. Le Guin's story, however, has a modern twist—it is narrated from the perspective of Eve, the first woman. In this brief tale, Le Guin's use of descriptive language enhances her perspectives on gender barriers, inequality, and identity.

"Most of them accepted namelessness . . ."

1   Most of them accepted namelessness with the perfect indifference with which they had so long accepted and ignored their names. Whales and dolphins, seals and sea otters consented with particular grace and **alacrity**, sliding into anonymity as into their element. A faction of yaks, however, protested. They said that "yak" sounded right, and that almost everyone who knew they existed called them that. Unlike the ubiquitous creatures such as rats and fleas, who had been called by hundreds or thousands of different names since Babel, the yaks could truly say, they said, that they had a *name*. They discussed the matter all summer. The councils of the elderly females finally agreed that though the name might be useful to others it was so redundant from the yak point of view that they never spoke it themselves and hence might as well dispense with it. After they presented the argument in this light to their bulls, a full consensus was delayed only by the onset of severe early blizzards. Soon after the beginning of the thaw, their agreement was reached and the designation "yak" was returned to the donor.

2   Among the domestic animals, few horses had cared what anybody called them since the failure of Dean Swift's[1] attempt to name them from their own vocabulary. Cattle, sheep, swine, asses, mules, and goats, along with chickens, geese, and turkeys, all agreed enthusiastically to give their names back to the people to whom—as they put it—they belonged.

3   A couple of problems did come up with pets. The cats, of course, **steadfastly** denied ever having had any name other than those self-given, unspoken, ineffably personal names which, as the poet Eliot[2] said, they spend long hours daily contemplating—though none of the contemplators has ever admitted that what they contemplate is their names and some onlookers have wondered if the object of that meditative gaze might not in fact be the Perfect, or Platonic, Mouse. In any case, it is a moot point now. It was with the dogs, and with some parrots, lovebirds, ravens, and mynahs, that the trouble arose. These verbally talented individuals insisted that their names were

NOTES

Skill:
Allusion

I know that Babel is a story in the Bible. I also know Adam gives all the animals their names in the Bible. I wonder if the animals losing their names has something to do with the story of Adam.

---

1. **Dean Swift** Anglo-Irish author Jonathan Swift, whose satirical novel *Gulliver's Travels* imagines a race of talking horses
2. **Eliot** American/British poet T.S. Eliot, who wrote the poem "The Naming of Cats"

important to them, and flatly refused to part with them. But as soon as they understood that the issue was precisely one of individual choice, and that anybody who wanted to be called Rover, or Froufrou, or Polly, or even Birdie in the personal sense, was perfectly free to do so, not one of them had the least objection to parting with the lowercase (or, as regards German creatures, uppercase) generic appellations "poodle," "parrot," "dog," or "bird," and all the Linnaean qualifiers that had trailed along behind them for two hundred years like tin cans tied to a tail.

4   The insects parted with their names in **vast** clouds and swarms of ephemeral syllables buzzing and stinging and humming and flitting and crawling and tunneling away.

5   As for the fish of the sea, their names dispersed from them in silence throughout the oceans like faint, dark blurs of cuttlefish ink, and drifted off on the currents without a trace.

**Skill:
Theme**

In this section I notice that by unnaming all the animals, Eve has changed her relationship with them. She thinks about how she feels closer to them because she has removed all of their labels. These thoughts show a theme that labels can be a barrier to equality.

6   NONE were left now to unname, and yet how close I felt to them when I saw one of them swim or fly or trot or crawl across my way or over my skin, or stalk me in the night, or go along beside me for a while in the day. They seemed far closer than when their names had stood between myself and them like a clear barrier: so close that my fear of them and their fear of me became one same fear. And the attraction that many of us felt, the desire to smell one another's smells, feel or rub or caress one another's scales or skin or feathers or fur, taste one another's blood or flesh, keep one another warm—that attraction was now all one with the fear, and the hunter could not be told from the hunted, nor the eater from the food.

7   This was more or less the effect I had been after. It was somewhat more powerful than I had anticipated, but I could not now, in all conscience, make an exception for myself. I **resolutely** put anxiety away, went to Adam, and said, "You and your father lent me this—gave it to me, actually. It's been really useful, but it doesn't exactly seem to fit very well lately. But thanks very much! It's really been very useful."

8   It is hard to give back a gift without sounding **peevish** or ungrateful, and I did not want to leave him with that impression of me. He was not paying much attention, as it happened, and said only, "Put it down over there, O.K.?" and went on with what he was doing.

9   One of my reasons for doing what I did was that talk was getting us nowhere, but all the same I felt a little let down. I had been prepared to defend my decision. And I thought that perhaps when he did notice he might be upset and want to talk. I put some things away and fiddled around a little, but he

Copyright © BookheadEd Learning, LLC

continued to do what he was doing and to take no notice of anything else. At last I said, "Well, goodbye, dear. I hope the garden key turns up."

10 He was fitting parts together, and said, without looking around, "O.K., fine, dear. When's dinner?"

11 "I'm not sure," I said. "I'm going now. With the—" I hesitated, and finally said, "With them, you know," and went on out. In fact, I had only just then realized how hard it would have been to explain myself. I could not chatter away as I used to do, taking it all for granted. My words now must be as slow, as new, as single, as tentative as the steps I took going down the path away from the house, between the dark-branched, tall dancers motionless against the winter shining.

Please note that excerpts and passages in the StudySync® library and this workbook are intended as touchstones to generate interest in an author's work. The excerpts and passages do not substitute for the reading of entire texts, and StudySync® strongly recommends that students seek out and purchase the whole literary or informational work in order to experience it as the author intended. Links to online resellers are available in our digital library. In addition, complete works may be ordered through an authorized reseller by filling out and returning to StudySync® the order form enclosed in this workbook.

Reading & Writing Companion   25

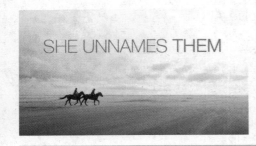

SHE UNNAMES THEM

First Read

Read "She Unnames Them." After you read, complete the Think Questions below.

 THINK QUESTIONS

1. What was the narrator's intention for "unnaming" the animals? Refer to paragraphs 6 and 7 and use evidence from the text to support your answer.

2. What can you infer about Adam and Eve's relationship? Use evidence from the last three paragraphs of the story to defend your answer.

3. Why did the narrator decide to leave Adam at the end of the story? Cite specific evidence from the text in your answer.

4. What is the meaning of the word **peevish** as it is used in the text? Write your best definition here, along with a brief explanation of how you arrived at its meaning.

5. Read the following dictionary entry:

vast
vast /vast/

adjective

1. of very great extent or quantity; immense

noun

2. an immense space

Use context to determine which of these definitions most closely matches the use of **vast** in "She Unnames Them." Write the definition here and explain how you figured it out.

Skill:
Allusion

Use the Checklist to analyze Allusion in "She Unnames Them." Refer to the sample student annotations about Allusion in the text.

••• CHECKLIST FOR ALLUSION

In order to identify an allusion, note the following:

- ✓ clues in a specific work that suggest a reference to previous source material

- ✓ when the author references previous source material

- ✓ the theme, event, character, or situation in a text to which the allusion adds information

To better understand the source material an author used to create a new work, do the following:

- ✓ use a print or digital resource to look up the work and any other allusions

- ✓ list details about the work or allusion that are related to the new work

To analyze how an author draws on and transforms source material in a specific work of fiction, consider the following questions:

- ✓ What theme/event/character from another work is referenced in the fiction I am reading? How do I know?

- ✓ How does that theme/event/character change or transform in this new text?

- ✓ What does the modern version of the story add to the earlier story?

Please note that excerpts and passages in the StudySync® library and this workbook are intended as touchstones to generate interest in an author's work. The excerpts and passages do not substitute for the reading of entire texts, and StudySync® strongly recommends that students seek out and purchase the whole literary or informational work in order to experience it as the author intended. Links to online resellers are available in our digital library. In addition, complete works may be ordered through an authorized reseller by filling out and returning to StudySync® the order form enclosed in this workbook.

Reading & Writing Companion   27

Skill:
Allusion

Reread paragraphs 7–9 of "She Unnames Them" and the excerpts from the text below. Then, write the letter for each Biblical allusion that best relates to the excerpt provided.

↻ YOUR TURN

	Excerpt Options
A	There is no clear allusion.
B	And Adam said, This is now bone of my bones, and flesh of my flesh: she shall be called Woman, because she was taken out of Man.
C	Therefore the Lord God sent him forth from the garden of Eden, to till the ground from whence he was taken.

Excerpt from "She Unnames Them"	Excerpt from the Bible
"You and your father lent me this – gave it to me, actually. It's been really useful, but it doesn't exactly seem to fit very well lately. But thanks very much! It's really been very useful."	
One of my reasons for doing what I did was that talk was getting us nowhere, but all the same I felt a little let down.	
At last I said, "Well, goodbye, dear. I hope the garden key turns up."	

Skill: Theme

Use the Checklist to analyze Theme in "She Unnames Them." Refer to the sample student annotations about Theme in the text.

••• CHECKLIST FOR THEME

In order to identify a theme or central idea of a text, note the following:

- ✓ the subject of the text and a theme that might be stated directly in the text

- ✓ details in the text that help to reveal theme

  - the title and chapter headings
  - details about the setting
  - the narrator's or speaker's tone
  - characters' thoughts, actions, and dialogue
  - the central conflict in a story's plot
  - the climax, or turning point in the story
  - the resolution of the conflict
  - changes in characters, setting, or plot events

- ✓ specific details that shape and refine the theme

To determine a theme or central idea of a text and analyze in detail its development over the course of the text, including how it emerges and is shaped and refined by specific details, consider the following questions:

- ✓ How do details of setting, characters, and plot events lead to a message about life?

- ✓ What is a theme of the text? How and when does it emerge?

- ✓ Is there more than one theme? How do I know?

- ✓ What specific details shape and refine the theme?

- ✓ How does each theme develop over the course of the text?

Skill:
Theme

Reread paragraphs 8–11 of "She Unnames Them." Then, using the Checklist on the previous page, answer the multiple-choice questions below.

⟳ YOUR TURN

1. This question has two parts. First, answer Part A. Then, answer Part B.

   Part A: Identify the theme that most clearly emerges from the details in the passage.

   ○ A. Achieving freedom sometimes requires us to enter into the unknown.

   ○ B. The transition from childhood to adulthood is often a sad one.

   ○ C. Leaving an important relationship behind can create a sense of grief and loss.

   ○ D. Language is a powerful force because it can unite us with others.

   Part B: Which of Eve's actions helps BEST to develop the theme identified in Part A?

   ○ A. She doubts her choice to leave her name and Adam behind.

   ○ B. She stops worrying about explaining her choices to others.

   ○ C. For the first time, Eve's fear overcomes her.

   ○ D. She feels more certain of how to express herself than ever.

Skill:
Compare and Contrast

Use the Checklist to analyze Compare and Contrast in "She Unnames Them."

••• CHECKLIST FOR COMPARE AND CONTRAST

In order to determine how to compare and contrast a text to its source material, use the following steps:

✓ First, choose works of literature in which the author draws on and transforms elements from another source, such as theme in John Green's *The Fault in Our Stars* and Shakespeare's *Romeo and Juliet*, or Ovid's poems on Greek and Roman mythology and their influence on Shakespeare.

✓ Next, identify literary elements that are comparable in the text and its source:

- the series of events that make up each plot

- connections between the characters and what motivates them

- the theme in each work

- the message or ideas the authors want to communicate to readers

✓ Finally, explain ways the author transforms the source material, perhaps by updating certain aspects of the plot or changing a character's traits.

To analyze how an author draws on and transforms source material in order to compare and contrast, consider the following questions:

✓ How does the author draw from the source material?

✓ How does the author transform the source material?

✓ How do the literary elements in the text compare to its source?

Skill:
Compare and Contrast

Reread paragraphs 9–11 from "She Unnames Them" and lines 14–23 from "I Am Offering This Poem." Then, using the Checklist on the previous page, complete the chart on the next page to compare and contrast the passages. Write the letter for each sentence in the correct column.

YOUR TURN

	Observation Options
A	Words matter to the narrator and speaker.
B	Words seem hard to say.
C	The words from the speaker to the recipient are warm and caring.
D	For the narrator and speaker, words are meaningful and powerful.
E	Both show a relationship between two people.
F	The relationship is a strong one.
G	Words flow easily.
H	The words between the narrator and her partner are distant and cold.
I	The relationship is ending.

"She Unnames Them"	Both	"I Am Offering This Poem"

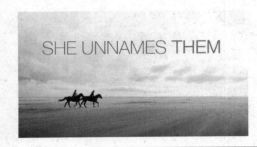

SHE UNNAMES THEM

Close Read

Reread "She Unnames Them." As you reread, complete the Skills Focus questions below. Then use your answers and annotations from the questions to help you complete the Write activity.

◎ SKILLS FOCUS

1. Discuss the ways in which Le Guin alludes to the Book of Genesis in the Bible and how she makes it new through her story.

2. Explain the main theme of "She Unnames Them" and describe how the specific details shape and refine the theme over the course of the story.

3. The narrator of "I Am Offering This Poem" says, in the final stanza,

   It's all I have to give,
   and all anyone needs to live,

   and to go on living inside,
   when the world outside
   no longer cares if you live or die;

   Explain what the narrator of "She Unnames Them" believes she is giving to the natural world, and why.

4. In Genesis in the Bible, Adam is tasked with naming all the animals. Explain why, based on Le Guin's story, Eve may want to use the power of words in a negative sense, by "unnaming."

✎ WRITE

COMPARE AND CONTRAST: Philosopher Suzanne K. Langer said, "The very notion of giving something a name was the vastest generative idea that was ever conceived." The plot of "She Unnames Them," which centers on the voluntary unnaming of Eve and the animals, plays an important role in communicating a theme concerning hierarchy. Using "She Unnames Them" and "I Am Offering This Poem" as sources, discuss how writers use language to develop themes and ideas and how those words give the themes and ideas power.

The Story of a Vision

FICTION
Francis La Flesche
1901

Introduction

Francis La Flesche (1857–1932) was the first Native American to work for the Smithsonian Institution as a professional anthropologist. His fiction and his ethnography offer invaluable documents of Omaha and Osage tribal cultures. Most of La Flesche's short stories, including "The Story of a Vision," are based on the rich folktales of the Omaha tribe that defined the author's childhood. La Flesche integrates the tribe's belief system into much of his writing—especially that of spirit, retribution, community, and omens—which makes "A Story of a Vision" that much more enchanting.

"In the old days, many strange things came to pass in the life of our people . . ."

1   Each of us, as we gathered at the lodge of our storyteller at dusk, picked up an armful of wood and entered. The old man who was sitting alone, his wife having gone on a visit, welcomed us with a pleasant word as we threw the wood down by the fire-place and busied ourselves rekindling the fire.

2   Ja-bae-ka and Ne-ne-ba, having nothing to do at this moment, fell to scuffling. "You will be fighting if you keep on," warned the old man.

3   "Stop your fooling and come and sit down," scolded Wa-du-pa. "You're not in your own house."

Omaha Dance

4   The flames livened up cheerily and cast a **ruddy** glow about us when Wa-du-pa said,

5   "Grandfather, the last time we were here, you told us the myth of the eagle and the wren; we liked it, but now we want a true story, something that really happened, something you saw yourself."

6   "How thirsty I am!" said the old man irrelevantly. "I wonder what makes me so dry."

7   "Quick!" said Wa-du-pa, motioning to Ja-bae-ka, "Get some water!"

8   The lad peered into one kettle, squinted into another, and then said, "There isn't any."

9   "Then go, get some!" arose a number of voices.

10   "Why don't some of you go?" Ja-bae-ka **retorted,** picking up one of the kettles.

11   "Take both!" someone shouted.

12   Ja-bae-ka approached the door grumbling. As he grasped the heavy skin portier to make his way out, he turned and said, "Don't begin until I come back."

NOTES

13   We soon heard his heavy breathing in the long entrance way. "It's moonlight, just like day!" he exclaimed, as he set the kettles down and thrust his cold hands into the flames with a twisting motion. "The boys and girls are having lots of fun sliding on the ice."

14   "Let them slide, we don't care!" ejaculated Wa-du-pa as he dipped a cup into the water and handed it to the old man, who put it to his lips and made a gulping sound as he drank, the lump in his throat leaping up and down at each swallow. At the last draught, he expelled his pent-up breath with something like a groan, set the cup down, wiped his lips with the back of his hand, and asked, "A real true story—something that I saw myself; that's what you want, is it?"

15   "Yes, grandfather," we sang out in chorus. "A story that has you in it!"

16   His face brightened with a smile and he broke into a gentle laugh, nodding his head to its rhythm.

17   After a few moments' **musing,** and when we boys had settled down, the old man began: "Many, many winters ago, long before any of you were born, our people went on a winter hunt, away out among the sand hills where even now we sometimes go. There was a misunderstanding between the leaders, so that just as we reached the hunting grounds the tribe separated into two parties, each going in a different direction.

18   "The weather was pleasant enough while on the journey, but a few days after the departure of our friends, a heavy storm came upon us. For days and nights the wind howled and roared, threatening to carry away our tents, and the snow fell thick and fast, so that we could not see an arm's length; it was waist deep and yet it kept falling. No hunting could be done; food grew scarcer and scarcer, and the older people became alarmed.

19   "One afternoon as my father, mother and I were sitting in our tent eating from our last kettle of corn, there came a lull and we heard with startling distinctness a man singing a song of augury. We paused to listen, but the wind swept down again and drowned the voice.

20   "'A holy man seeking for a sign,' said my father. 'Son, go and hear if he will give us words of courage.'

21   "My father was lame and could not go himself, so I waded through the heavy drifts and with much difficulty reached the man's tent, where many were already gathered to hear the predictions. I held my breath in awe as I heard the holy man say:

22 "'For a moment the wind ceased to blow, the clouds parted, and in the rift I saw standing, in mid air against the blue sky, the spirit of the man who was murdered last summer. His head was bowed in grief and although he spoke not, I know from the vision that the anger of the storm gods was moved against us for not punishing the murderer. Silently the spirit lifted an arm and pointed beyond the hills. Then I found that I too was in midair. I looked over the hilltops and beheld a forest, where shadowy forms like those of large animals moved among the trees. I turned once more to the spirit, but the clouds had come together again.

23 "'Before dawn to-morrow the storm will pass away, then let the runners go to the forest that I saw and tell us whether or not there is truth in the words that I have spoken.'

24 "As predicted, the wind ceased to blow and the snow to fall. Runners were hastily sent to the forest, and the sun was hardly risen when one of them returned with the good news that the shadowy forms the holy man had seen were truly those of buffalo.

25 "The effect of the news upon the camp was like magic, faces brightened, the gloomy **forebodings** that clouded the minds of the older people fled as did the storm, and laughter and pleasantries enlivened the place. The hunters and boys were soon plodding through the snow toward the forest, and before dark every one returned heavily laden, tired and hungry, but nonetheless happy. The fires burned brightly that night, and men told stories until it was nearly morning.

26 "The forest of the vision was a bag of game; every few days the hunters went there and returned with buffalo, elk, or deer, so that even the poorest man had plenty for his wife and children to eat.

27 "All this time nothing had been heard from the party that separated from us before the storm. One night when I came home from a rabbit hunt, I found my mother and father packing up pemican and jerked meat as though for a journey. I looked inquiringly at the pack as I ate my supper; bye and bye my mother told me that a man had just come from the other camp with the news that the people had exhausted their supplies and, as they could find no game, they were suffering for want of food. My sister and her husband were in that camp, and I was told to carry the pack to them.

28 "My father had arranged with a young man bound on a similar errand to call for me early in the morning, so I went to bed as soon as I had finished eating to get as much sleep and rest as possible. It was well that I did, for long before dawn creaking footsteps approached our tent and the man called out, 'Are you ready?' I quickly slipped on my leggings and moccasins, put on my robe, slung the pack over my shoulders, and we started.

29 "To avoid the drifts, we followed the ridges, but even there the snow lay deep, and we were continually breaking through the hard crust. My friend turned every mishap into a joke and broke the **monotony** of our travel with humorous tales and incidents. Late at night we camped in the bend of a small, wooded stream. We gathered a big pile of dry branches, kindled a roaring fire, and roasted some of the jerked meat. When supper was over, we dried our moccasins, then piling more wood on the fire, we wrapped ourselves up in our robes and went to sleep.

30 "I do not know how long we might have slept had we not been wakened by the howling of hundreds of wolves not far away from us. 'They're singing to the morning star!' said my friend. 'It is near day, so we must be up and going.'

31 "We ate a little of the pemican, helped each other to load, and again we started. Before night we were overtaken by other men and boys who were also going to the relief of their friends in the other camp, where we arrived just in time to save many of the people from starving.

32 "How curious it was that the predictions of the holy man should come true—the stopping of the storm before morning, the forest, and the shadowy forms of animals. Stranger still was the death of the murderer. This took place, we were told by the people we had rescued, on the very night of the augury in our camp. They said, as the man was sitting in his tent that night, the wind suddenly blew the door flap violently aside, an expression of terror came over his face, he fell backward, and he was dead.

33 "In the old days, many strange things came to pass in the life of our people, but now we are getting to be different."

34 Wa-du-pa thanked the storyteller, and we were about to go when Ne-ne-ba, pointing to Ja-bae-ka, whispered, "He's gone to sleep! Let's scare him."

35 The old man fell into the spirit of the fun, so we all tip-toed to the back part of the lodge where it was dark and watched, as the flames died down to a blue flickering. We could see the boy's head drop lower and lower until his nose nearly touched his knee. Just then a log on the fire suddenly tumbled from its place, broke in two, sent up a shower of crackling sparks, and Ja-bae-ka awoke with a start. He threw up his head, looked all around, and thinking he was left alone in the darkened lodge, took fright and rushed to the door with a cry of terror. We ran out of our hiding places with shouts of laughter and overtook Ja-bae-ka outside the door, where we teased him about going to sleep and being afraid in the dark.

36 Suddenly he turned upon Ne-ne-ba and said, "You did that, you rascal! I'll pay you back sometime."

WRITE

LITERARY ANALYSIS: In this short story, the Grandfather relates a story in order to convey an important life lesson to the youth of his tribe. Determine and analyze the theme of this story, including how the theme emerges and is shaped by details of character and setting.

Heart of Darkness

FICTION
Joseph Conrad
1899

Introduction

P rior to his career as an author, Joseph Conrad (1857–1924) was a member of both the French and British naval forces. His experiences as a sailor and seaman included journeys to India, Australia, and Africa—and it was during these travels that Conrad became inspired to write about the horrors of colonialism. One of his most controversial and memorable works, *Heart of Darkness* is derived from his time in the Congo Free State, ruled at the time by King Leopold II of Belgium, where Conrad purportedly came face-to-face with the depths of madness found in colonialism, the African jungle, and the human psyche. The story follows river-boat captain Charles Marlow along the Congo River in his pursuit of ivory, a journey that brings him into contact with cannibals, crazed traders, and the enigmatic, rogue agent, Kurtz.

"We penetrated deeper and deeper into the heart of darkness."

Copyright © BookheadEd Learning, LLC

NOTES

from Chapter II

1   "It's a wonder to me yet. Imagine a blindfolded man set to drive a van over a bad road. I sweated and shivered over that business considerably, I can tell you. After all, for a seaman, to scrape the bottom of the thing that's supposed to float all the time under his care is the unpardonable sin. No one may know of it, but you never forget the thump—eh? A blow on the very heart. You remember it, you dream of it, you wake up at night and think of it—years after—and go hot and cold all over. I don't pretend to say that steamboat floated all the time. More than once she had to wade for a bit, with twenty cannibals splashing around and pushing. We had enlisted some of these chaps on the way for a crew. Fine fellows—cannibals—in their place. They were men one could work with, and I am grateful to them. And, after all, they did not eat each other before my face: they had brought along a **provision** of hippo-meat which went rotten, and made the mystery of the wilderness stink in my nostrils. Phoo! I can sniff it now. I had the manager on board and three or four pilgrims with their staves—all complete. Sometimes we came upon a station close by the bank, clinging to the skirts of the unknown, and the white men rushing out of a tumble-down hovel, with great gestures of joy and surprise and welcome, seemed very strange,—had the appearance of being held there captive by a spell. The word ivory would ring in the air for a while— and on we went again into the silence, along empty reaches, round the still bends, between the high walls of our winding way, reverberating in hollow claps the ponderous beat of the stern-wheel. Trees, trees, millions of trees, massive, immense, running up high; and at their foot, hugging the bank against the stream, crept the little begrimed steamboat, like a sluggish beetle crawling on the floor of a lofty portico. It made you feel very small, very lost, and yet it was not altogether depressing, that feeling. After all, if you were small, the grimy beetle crawled on—which was just what you wanted it to do. Where the pilgrims imagined it crawled to I don't know. To some place where they expected to get something, I bet! For me it crawled toward Kurtz— exclusively; but when the steam-pipes started leaking we crawled very slow. The reaches opened before us and closed behind, as if the forest had stepped leisurely across the water to bar the way for our return. We penetrated deeper and deeper into the heart of darkness. It was very quiet there. At

night sometimes the roll of drums behind the curtain of trees would run up the river and remain sustained faintly, as if hovering in the air high over our heads, till the first break of day. Whether it meant war, peace, or prayer we could not tell. The dawns were heralded by the descent of a chill stillness; the woodcutters slept, their fires burned low; the snapping of a twig would make you start. We were wanderers on a prehistoric earth, on an earth that wore the aspect of an unknown planet. We could have fancied ourselves the first of men taking possession of an accursed inheritance, to be subdued at the cost of **profound** anguish and of excessive toil. But suddenly, as we struggled round a bend, there would be a glimpse of rush walls, of peaked grass-roofs, a burst of yells, a whirl of black limbs, a mass of hands clapping, of feet stamping, of bodies swaying, of eyes rolling, under the droop of heavy and motionless foliage. The steamer toiled along slowly on the edge of a black and incomprehensible frenzy. The prehistoric man was cursing us, praying to us, welcoming us—who could tell? We were cut off from the comprehension of our surroundings; we glided past like phantoms, wondering and secretly appalled, as sane men would be before an enthusiastic outbreak in a madhouse. We could not understand, because we were too far and could not remember, because we were traveling in the night of first ages, of those ages that are gone, leaving hardly a sign—and no memories.

2 "The earth seemed unearthly. We are accustomed to look upon the shackled form of a conquered monster, but there—there you could look at a thing monstrous and free. It was unearthly, and the men were—No, they were not inhuman. Well, you know, that was the worst of it—this suspicion of their not being inhuman. It would come slowly to one. They howled, and leaped, and spun, and made horrid faces; but what thrilled you was just the thought of their humanity—like yours—the thought of your remote kinship with this wild and passionate uproar. Ugly. Yes, it was ugly enough; but if you were man enough you would admit to yourself that there was in you just the faintest trace of a response to the terrible frankness of that noise, a dim suspicion of there being a meaning in it which you—you so remote from the night of first ages—could comprehend. And why not? The mind of man is capable of anything—because everything is in it, all the past as well as all the future. What was there after all? Joy, fear, sorrow, devotion, valor, rage—who can tell?—but truth—truth stripped of its cloak of time. Let the fool gape and shudder—the man knows, and can look on without a wink. But he must at least be as much of a man as these on the shore. He must meet that truth with his own true stuff—with his own inborn strength. Principles? Principles won't do. **Acquisitions**, clothes, pretty rags— rags that would fly off at the first good shake. No; you want a deliberate belief. An appeal to me in this fiendish row—is there? Very well; I hear; I admit, but I have a voice too, and for good or evil mine is the speech that cannot be silenced. Of course, a fool, what with sheer fright and fine sentiments, is always safe. Who's that grunting? You wonder I didn't go ashore for a howl and a dance? Well, no—I didn't. Fine sentiments, you say? Fine sentiments, be

Please note that excerpts and passages in the StudySync® library and this workbook are intended as touchstones to generate interest in an author's work. The excerpts and passages do not substitute for the reading of entire texts, and StudySync® strongly recommends that students seek out and purchase the whole literary or informational work in order to experience it as the author intended. Links to online resellers are available in our digital library. In addition, complete works may be ordered through an authorized reseller by filling out and returning to StudySync® the order form enclosed in this workbook.

Reading & Writing Companion   **43**

hanged! I had no time. I had to mess about with white-lead and strips of woolen blanket helping to put bandages on those leaky steam-pipes—I tell you. I had to watch the steering, and **circumvent** those snags, and get the tin-pot along by hook or by crook. There was surface-truth enough in these things to save a wiser man. And between whiles I had to look after the savage who was fireman. He was an improved specimen; he could fire up a vertical boiler. He was there below me, and, upon my word, to look at him was as edifying as seeing a dog in a parody of breeches and a feather hat, walking on his hind-legs. A few months of training had done for that really fine chap. He squinted at the steam-gauge and at the water-gauge with an evident effort of intrepidity—and he had filed teeth too, the poor devil, and the wool of his pate shaved into queer patterns, and three ornamental scars on each of his cheeks. He ought to have been clapping his hands and stamping his feet on the bank, instead of which he was hard at work, a thrall to strange witchcraft, full of improving knowledge. He was useful because he had been instructed; and what he knew was this—that should the water in that transparent thing disappear, the evil spirit inside the boiler would get angry through the greatness of his thirst, and take a terrible vengeance. So he sweated and fired up and watched the glass fearfully (with an **impromptu** charm, made of rags, tied to his arm, and a piece of polished bone, as big as a watch, stuck flatways through his lower lip), while the wooded banks slipped past us slowly, the short noise was left behind, the interminable miles of silence—and we crept on, towards Kurtz. But the snags were thick, the water was **treacherous** and shallow, the boiler seemed indeed to have a sulky devil in it, and thus neither that fireman nor I had any time to peer into our creepy thoughts.

✏ WRITE

LITERARY ANALYSIS: *Heart of Darkness* is narrated from the perspective of a European exploring Africa. The passage conveys his perspective on his journey into the unknown as he experiences new regions of the globe. How does the author characterize the narrator through the historical setting? In your response, cite textual evidence to support your analysis.

Things Fall Apart

FICTION
Chinua Achebe
1958

Introduction

Nigerian writer and Igbo chieftain Chinua Achebe (1930–2013) was a towering figure in African literature. Achebe's writing captures the traditional rhythms of his West African ancestors through language and dialogue; his works focus mainly on African identity, the effects of colonialism, and the preservation of culture. *Things Fall Apart*, his 1958 masterwork, tells the story of Okonkwo, the well-respected leader of a Nigerian village until—as the title would suggest—things take a turn for the worse. In this excerpt from the first chapter, readers are introduced to a father and son who are very different from one another.

"... Okonkwo's fame had grown like a bush-fire ..."

NOTES

Chapter One

1   Okonkwo was well known throughout the nine villages and even beyond. His fame rested on solid personal achievements. As a young man of eighteen he had brought honor to his village by throwing Amalinze the Cat. Amalinze was the great wrestler who for seven years was unbeaten, from Umuofia to Mbaino. He was called the Cat because his back would never touch the earth. It was this man that Okonkwo threw in a fight which the old men agreed was one of the fiercest since the founder of their town engaged a spirit of the wild for seven days and seven nights.

2   The drums beat and the flutes sang and the **spectators** held their breath. Amalinze was a wily craftsman, but Okonkwo was as slippery as a fish in water. Every nerve and every muscle stood out on their arms, on their backs and their thighs, and one almost heard them stretching to breaking point. In the end, Okonkwo threw the Cat.

3   That was many years ago, twenty years or more, and during this time Okonkwo's fame had grown like a bush-fire in the harmattan. He was tall and huge, and his bushy eyebrows and wide nose gave him a very **severe** look. He breathed heavily, and it was said that, when he slept, his wives and children in their houses could hear him breathe. When he walked, his heels hardly touched the ground and he seemed to walk on springs, as if he was going to pounce on somebody. And he did pounce on people quite often. He had a slight stammer and whenever he was angry and could not get his words out quickly enough, he would use his fists. He had no patience with unsuccessful men. He had had no patience with his father.

4   Unoka, for that was his father's name, had died ten years ago. In his day he was lazy and **improvident** and was quite incapable of thinking about tomorrow. If any money came his way, and it seldom did, he immediately bought gourds of palm-wine, called round his neighbors and made merry. He always said that whenever he saw a dead man's mouth he saw the folly of not eating what one had in one's lifetime. Unoka was, of course, a debtor,

Skill:
Theme

Okonkwo's father was irresponsible. However, I infer that Unoka had worth: he liked joy. I see a theme about the difficulty of reconciling a parent's good and bad traits.

Copyright © BookheadEd Learning, LLC

and he owed every neighbor some money, from a few cowries to quite substantial amounts.

5   He was tall but very thin and had a slight stoop. He wore a **haggard** and mournful look except when he was drinking or playing on his flute. He was very good on his flute, and his happiest moments were the two or three moons after the harvest when the village musicians brought down their instruments, hung above the fireplace. Unoka would play with them, his face beaming with blessedness and peace. Sometimes another village would ask Unoka's band and their dancing egwugwu[1] to come and stay with them and teach them their tunes. They would go to such hosts for as long as three or four markets, making music and feasting. Unoka loved the good fare and the good fellowship, and he loved this season of the year, when the rains had stopped and the sun rose every morning with dazzling beauty. And it was not too hot either, because the cold and dry harmattan wind was blowing down from the north. Some years the harmattan was very severe and a **dense** haze hung on the atmosphere. Old men and children would then sit round log fires, warming their bodies. Unoka loved it all, and he loved the first kites that returned with the dry season, and the children who sang songs of welcome to them. He would remember his own childhood, how he had often wandered around looking for a kite sailing leisurely against the blue sky. As soon as he found one he would sing with his whole being, welcoming it back from its long, long journey, and asking it if it had brought home any lengths of cloth.

6   That was years ago, when he was young. Unoka, the grown-up, was a failure. He was poor and his wife and children had barely enough to eat. People laughed at him because he was a loafer, and they swore never to lend him any more money because he never paid back. But Unoka was such a man that he always succeeded in borrowing more, and piling up his debts.

Excerpted from *Things Fall Apart* by Chinua Achebe, published by Anchor Books.

Skill:
Point of View

Although Okonkwo's father Unoka is a debtor, he is accepted and welcomed into surrounding villages for his talent with music during plentiful times of the year. He finds great joy in playing his flute, and his life is tied to the natural cycles of the land and harvest in a way that isn't common in the U.S. anymore. The story continues to be told from an outsider's perspective.

---

1. **egwugwu** masked elders of the community who represent ancestral gods

First Read

Read *Things Fall Apart*. After you read, complete the Think Questions below.

☁ THINK QUESTIONS

1. According to the narrator, Okonkwo "had no patience with unsuccessful men." What do you think is Okonkwo's definition of success? Support your answer with evidence from the text.

2. Explain what the following sentence reveals about Unoka's priorities: "He always said that whenever he saw a dead man's mouth he saw the folly of not eating what one had in one's lifetime." Refer to details from the text to support your answer.

3. What can you infer about the relationship between father and son when Unoka was alive? Support your answer with evidence that is directly stated as well as with ideas you have gathered from clues in the text.

4. Use context clues to determine the meaning of the word **haggard** as it is used in *Things Fall Apart*. Write your definition of *haggard* here and explain how you figured it out.

5. Read the following dictionary entry:

   dense
   dense / dens/

   adjective

   1. unintelligent; slow to learn or comprehend
   2. difficult to understand due to complexity of ideas, especially in a text
   3. being closely packed together so that it is difficult to move or see through

   Decide which definition best matches **dense** as it is used in *Things Fall Apart*. Write that definition of *dense* here and indicate which clues from the text helped you determine the meaning.

Skill:
Theme

Use the Checklist to analyze Theme in *Things Fall Apart*. Refer to the sample student annotations about Theme in the text.

••• CHECKLIST FOR THEME

In order to identify a theme or central idea of a text, note the following:

- ✓ the subject of the text and a theme that might be stated directly in the text

- ✓ details in the text that help to reveal theme

  - • the title and chapter headings
  - • details about the setting
  - • the narrator's or speaker's tone
  - • characters' thoughts, actions, and dialogue
  - • the central conflict in a story's plot
  - • the climax, or turning point in the story
  - • the resolution of the conflict
  - • shifts in characters, setting, or plot events

- ✓ specific details that shape and refine the theme

To determine a theme or central idea of a text and analyze in detail its development over the course of the text, including how it emerges and is shaped and refined by specific details, consider the following questions:

- ✓ What is a theme of the text? How and when does it emerge?

- ✓ What specific details shape and refine the theme?

- ✓ How does the theme develop over the course of the text?

Skill:
Theme

Reread paragraph 6 of *Things Fall Apart*. Then, using the Checklist on the previous page, answer the multiple-choice questions below.

⟳ YOUR TURN

1. What does paragraph 6 suggest most clearly about Unoka's personality?

   ○ A. He grew more amusing as he got older.
   ○ B. He was finally forced to work for his livelihood.
   ○ C. He was seen as more of a burden to those around him.
   ○ D. He lost the ability to talk people into lending him money.

2. From the evidence in paragraph 6, what inference can you make most clearly about Okonkwo's childhood?

   ○ A. Okonkwo grew up eager to follow in his father's footsteps.
   ○ B. Okonkwo felt ashamed of his father's lifestyle.
   ○ C. Okonkwo vowed to repay his father's many debts.
   ○ D. Okonkwo was thin and weak from lack of food.

3. The contrast between father and son supports the theme that—

   ○ A. children tend to be stronger and more successful than their parents.
   ○ B. we are often labeled with the reputation that our parents had.
   ○ C. family relationships have a strong effect on our worldview.
   ○ D. children of failures are less likely to work hard or save money.

Skill:
Point of View

Use the Checklist to analyze Point of View in *Things Fall Apart*. Refer to the sample student annotations about Point of View in the text.

In order to identify the point of view or cultural experience reflected in a work of literature from outside the United States, note the following:

- ✓ the pronouns the narrator or speaker uses

- ✓ what the narrator or speaker knows and reveals

- ✓ the country of origin of the characters and author

- ✓ moments in the work that reflect a cultural experience not common in the United States by drawing on reading from world literature, such as

  - • a drama written by Ibsen or Chekov or other international authors

  - • a story that reflects an indigenous person's experience in another country

To analyze the point of view or a cultural experience reflected in a work of literature from outside the United States, drawing on a wide reading of world literature, consider the following questions:

- ✓ What is the country of origin of the author of the text? Of the characters in the text?

- ✓ What texts have you read previously from these nations or cultures? How does this help you analyze the point of view of this text?

- ✓ How does this text use point of view to present a different cultural experience than that of the United States?

Skill:
Point of View

Reread paragraphs 2 and 3 of *Things Fall Apart.* Then, using the Checklist on the previous page, answer the multiple-choice questions below.

↻ YOUR TURN

1. What does this excerpt suggest about the importance of wrestling and strength in the setting of *Things Fall Apart*?

   ○ A. Wrestling is considered an inferior sport that is looked down upon greatly.

   ○ B. Wrestling used to be very important, but in the decades since Okonkwo defeated Amalinze people have stopped caring as much.

   ○ C. Being a strong wrestling champion is a widely respected feat.

   ○ D. Okonkwo is famed for his patience and strength.

2. Who is the narrator, and are there any clues as to his or her perspective on the story?

   ○ A. Unoka, Okonkwo's father, is the narrator, and he is disappointed that his son never had any patience for him.

   ○ B. The narrator is anonymous. The knowledge of Okonkwo's emotions and rumors about his family suggest an omniscient narrator.

   ○ C. Okonkwo is narrating, and he felt ashamed of his father's lifestyle.

   ○ D. The narrator is European and exploring villages in Africa for the first time.

Close Read

Reread *Things Fall Apart*. As you reread, complete the Skills Focus questions below. Then use your answers and annotations from the questions to help you complete the Write activity.

◎ SKILLS FOCUS

1. Discuss details from the opening of this novel that suggest experiences specific to a particular culture outside the United States.

2. Identify clues that suggest that Unoka was "an unsuccessful man." Using these details, explain what it means to be successful in the Igbo culture and how this develops a theme.

3. The title of Achebe's novel comes from a poem called "The Second Coming" written by Irish poet William Butler Yeats. In the poem the speaker says,

   Things fall apart; the centre cannot hold;
   Mere anarchy is loosed upon the world,. . .

   Based on this excerpt, discuss why Achebe may have alluded to Yeats's poem in his title.

4. Consider what it means to be a man in *Things Fall Apart* and in *Heart of Darkness*. Then explain how Okonkwo, Marlow, and the other male characters are similar in their show of masculinity—and how Unoka is different.

5. In the Native American story "The Story of a Vision," the storyteller says, "In the old days, many strange things came to pass in the life of our people, but now we are getting to be different." Explain how the narrators of *Heart of Darkness* and *Things Fall Apart* use language to develop themes around what is strange, different, or incomprehensible.

✏ WRITE

LITERARY ANALYSIS: Compare related themes in *Heart of Darkness* and *Things Fall Apart* about masculinity. Respond by analyzing how the authors represent different cultural perspectives and what the details reveal about the worlds the characters live in.

My Grandmother Washes Her Feet in the Sink of the Bathroom at Sears

POETRY
Mohja Kahf
2003

Introduction

Five times a day, it is the duty of a practicing Muslim to answer the ritual call to prayer. But in the big box stores of the American Midwest, this can get a little complicated. In this poem by Syrian American writer Mohja Kahf (b. 1967), the speaker explores, from a distinctly Arab American perspective, what happens when a clash of civilizations occurs in the bathroom of a department store.

"I can see a clash of civilizations brewing in the Sears bathroom"

1 My grandmother puts her feet in the sink
2 of the bathroom at Sears
3 to wash them in the **ritual** washing for prayer,
4 *wudu*,
5 because she has to pray in the store or miss
6 the **mandatory** prayer time for Muslims
7 She does it with great poise, balancing
8 herself with one plump matronly arm
9 against the automated hot-air hand dryer,
10 after having removed her support knee-highs
11 and laid them aside, folded in thirds,
12 and given me her purse and her packages to hold
13 so she can accomplish this august ritual
14 and get back to the ritual of shopping for housewares

15 Respectable Sears **matrons** shake their heads and frown
16 as they notice what my grandmother is doing,
17 an affront to American porcelain,
18 a contamination of American Standards[1]
19 by something foreign and unhygienic
20 requiring civic action and possible use of disinfectant spray
21 They fluster about and flutter their hands and I can see
22 a clash of **civilizations** brewing in the Sears bathroom

23 My grandmother, though she speaks no English,
24 catches their meaning and her look in the mirror says,
25 *I have washed my feet over Iznik tile in Istanbul*
26 *with water from the world's ancient irrigation systems*
27 *I have washed my feet in the bathhouses of Damascus[2]*
28 *over painted bowls imported from China*
29 *among the best families of Aleppo[3]*

---

1. **American Standard** a brand that manufactures kitchen and bathroom plumbing fixtures
2. **Damascus** the capital of Syria
3. **Aleppo** the most populous city in Syria

Reading & Writing Companion

30 *And if you Americans knew anything*
31 *about civilization and cleanliness,*
32 *you'd make wider washbasins, anyway*
33 My grandmother knows one **culture**—the right one,

34 as do these matrons of the Middle West. For them,
35 my grandmother might as well have been squatting
36 in the mud over a rusty tin in vaguely tropical squalor,
37 Mexican or Middle Eastern, it doesn't matter which,
38 when she lifts her well-groomed foot and puts it over the edge.
39 "You can't do that," one of the women protests,
40 turning to me, "Tell her she can't do that."
41 "We wash our feet five times a day,"
42 my grandmother declares hotly in Arabic.
43 "My feet are cleaner than their sink.
44 Worried about their sink, are they? I
45 should worry about my feet!"
46 My grandmother nudges me, "Go on, tell them."

47 Standing between the door and the mirror, I can see
48 at multiple angles, my grandmother and the other shoppers,
49 all of them decent and goodhearted women, diligent
50 in cleanliness, grooming, and **decorum**
51 Even now my grandmother, not to be rushed,
52 is delicately drying her pumps with tissues from her purse
53 For my grandmother always wears well-turned pumps
54 that match her purse, I think in case someone
55 from one of the best families of Aleppo
56 should run into her—here, in front of the Kenmore display

57 I smile at the midwestern women
58 as if my grandmother has just said something lovely about them
59 and shrug at my grandmother as if they
60 had just apologized through me
61 No one is fooled, but I

62 hold the door open for everyone
63 and we all emerge on the sales floor
64 and lose ourselves in the great common ground
65 of housewares on markdown.

"My Grandmother Washes Her Feet in the Sink of the Bathroom at Sears," in *E-mails from Scheherazad,* by Mohja Kahf. Gainesville: University Press of Florida, 2003, pp. 26–28. Reprinted with permission of the University Press of Florida.

WRITE

PERSONAL RESPONSE: In "My Grandmother Washes Her Feet in the Sink of the Bathroom at Sears," the speaker feels conflicted about two sets of cultural expectations. Write a personal narrative about a time you felt stuck between two sets of expectations. In your personal narrative, describe the conflict, what you felt about the dynamic, and how you responded.

Please note that excerpts and passages in the StudySync® library and this workbook are intended as touchstones to generate interest in an author's work. The excerpts and passages do not substitute for the reading of entire texts, and StudySync® strongly recommends that students seek out and purchase the whole literary or informational work in order to experience it as the author intended. Links to online resellers are available in our digital library. In addition, complete works may be ordered through an authorized reseller by filling out and returning to StudySync® the order form enclosed in this workbook.

Reading & Writing
Companion

57

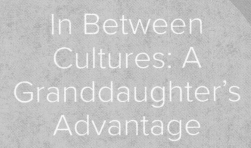

In Between Cultures: A Granddaughter's Advantage

ARGUMENTATIVE TEXT
Hayan Charara
2018

Introduction

Hayan Charara (b. 1972) is a Lebanese American poet, essayist, children's book author and editor whose work explores themes of Arab American identity, family, and culture. In this essay, Charara takes a close look at "My Grandmother Washes Her Feet in the Sink of the Bathroom at Sears" by Syrian American author Mohja Kahf. In Kahf's poem, the speaker explores, from a distinctly Arab American perspective, what happens when a clash of civilizations occurs in the bathroom of a department store. Charara explores Kahf's representation of the speaker's "in-between" identity and supports the poet's position that a life lived in-between yields great insight and understanding.

"Mirrors reflect ourselves back to us, helping to reveal what we might otherwise overlook."

1 For over a century Americans have been making choices at Sears. GE or Frigidaire? White or stainless steel? Extended warranty or take your chances? Likewise, the speaker in Mohja Kahf's "My Grandmother Washes Her Feet in the Sink of the Bathroom at Sears" must choose from a host of available **options**, not the least of which is "a clash of civilizations" or "the great common ground." Through her portrayal of the granddaughter, Kahf challenges the commonly held belief that hyphenated Americans are torn between two cultures.

NOTES

2 Confronted by customers who "shake their heads and frown" at her grandmother, who washes her feet in preparation for prayer, the speaker becomes an intermediary between two sides, East and West, each of which "knows one culture—the right one." The speaker must reconcile seemingly irreconcilable **perspectives**: on the one hand, that of the customers, who view the grandmother's act as "an affront to American porcelain, / a contamination of American Standards," and on the other hand, that of the grandmother herself, who, "though she speaks no English, / catches their meaning," takes offense, and, in Arabic, asks her granddaughter to hurl a "hotly" declared retort:

3 "My feet are cleaner than their sink.
Worried about their sink, are they? I
should worry about my feet!"

4 The granddaughter keeps this indignant response to herself. Her goal is to de-escalate the conflict, if not altogether resolve it, a task complicated by her identity. She belongs not to one or the other side, but to a bit of both. She is Arab and American, "foreign" and domestic. She literally stands in the middle, "between the door and the mirror," a difficult position to be in, for sure, one in which a person may feel torn. But doors not only close off spaces; they open into them. Mirrors reflect ourselves back to us, helping to reveal what we might otherwise overlook. In this way, the granddaughter's in-between identity provides her with a unique perspective—she sees both sides—and this proves to be advantageous.

5   Though tense, the drama between the grandmother and customers hardly rises to the level of epic conflict between cultures, and while a divide does exist between the two sides, it is not a chasm—the disagreement is grounded in lack of understanding, lack of knowledge, and lack of familiarity, which are not insurmountable obstacles. The women, in fact, have much in common. The speaker recognizes this, even if the women do not. For instance, both the grandmother and the women present themselves (and are represented by the speaker) as dignified women, "all of them decent and goodhearted." Despite their differences, cultural or otherwise, both sides also value "cleanliness, grooming, and decorum." And last but not least, both the grandmother and the "matrons" practice the same distinctive American act of consumerism—not Islam or Christianity, but a secular faith, one that welcomes adherents of all stripes, regardless of race, class, ethnicity, or even religious persuasion. As for consumerism, Sears is one of its oldest sects, replete with houses of worship (department stores), observances (blowout sales and holiday events), rules and obligations (see return policy on the back of your receipt), and even a "sacred" text (the Sears catalog). Whatever the grandmother and "matrons" do not know about each other's cultures, customs, or rituals, they know how to be good consumers. This unites them. It will be "housewares on markdown" that they lose themselves in, and they will come together "on the sales floor."

6   If anyone deserves credit for this coming together, however, it is not Sears, Roebuck, and Company, it is the granddaughter. Her in-between identity plays a central role in the bridge-building taking place. The granddaughter is a hyphenated American, perhaps American-born, certainly reared long enough in the United States as to be recognized by the matrons as American, or American enough. Not so with the grandmother, whose look (is she wearing a hijab?) and/or behavior (the sink incident) mark her as not American and definitely not American enough. For this reason, when one of the matrons protests the grandmother's **perceived** breach of bathroom etiquette, the woman turns immediately to the granddaughter to translate the demand, "Tell her she can't do that." The matron presumes that the grandmother "speaks no English" (she is right) but, more significantly, she assumes that the granddaughter does. The poet gives no explanation for why, so we can only guess. Perhaps the granddaughter is not visibly Muslim (no hijab?) or she simply acts more "American" (she doesn't wash her feet in a sink?). Whatever the reason, the matrons judge the granddaughter to be approachable, to be more like them than not. They regard her as a go-between.

7   So, too, does the grandmother. The grandmother also uses the granddaughter as a mediator, nudging her to "Go on, tell them." The back-and-forth between grandmother and matrons transforms the Sears bathroom into a mini-United

Nations. At the center of the debate between East and West is the granddaughter, a member of two cultures: one supposedly foreign, the other domestic. Historically, the granddaughter's predicament has been viewed as disadvantageous: she is stuck between a rock and a hard place, caught or trapped between cultures. Like generations of immigrants before her, she may feel pressure to overcome the difference, to choose sides—to assimilate.

8   That being so, the impulse may be to view the granddaughter's in-betweenness as unenviable: But this would be a mistake. In *Reflections On Exile*, Edward W. Said points out:

9   "Most people are principally aware of one culture, one setting, one home; exiles are aware of at least two, and this plurality of vision gives rise to an awareness of simultaneous dimensions, an awareness that is—to borrow a phrase from music—contrapuntal[1]."

10   Viewed from this perspective, the granddaughter holds an advantage over her grandmother and the matrons. In embracing her in-between **status**, her vision of the world shifts from being singular to plural. She can articulate and inhabit more than one culture, and she moves freely between them, between the "foreign" and domestic, planting her feet firmly on either side of the border. She speaks Arabic and English simultaneously, she negotiates linguistic and cultural differences effortlessly, and she code-switches freely ("sink" to "washbasin," "the ritual washing for prayer" to "*wudu,*" "bathhouses" to "bathrooms"). At the poem's end, it is difficult to imagine a reader feeling uneasy with how the grandmother uses the bathroom sink. At the very least, the act can no longer be seen as unhygienic or warranting cultural warfare. This is because of the granddaughter, who acts as an intermediary for the matrons, the grandmother, and the reader.

11   Ultimately, the granddaughter is neither foreign nor domestic. She is somewhere between. We use a variety of terms to describe people in this position, including *foreigner, exile, refugee, immigrant,* and *descendant of immigrants*. Uncomfortable though the role may be at times—especially during a confrontation in a public bathroom—the granddaughter takes it up without hesitation. In fact, she appears to relish her in-betweenness. Such positioning (as in-between cultures) allows the speaker insight that is lost on her grandmother and the matrons. *They* are so sure of their one right culture, that they appear to be stuck and at a disadvantage. In her role as intermediary, the granddaughter uses a simple gesture and a smile to resolve the conflict. She "hold[s] the door open for everyone" and creates a common ground without having to utter a single word. The women are finally able to "lose" their preconceived notions about one another and **emerge** together onto

---

1. **contrapuntal** in music, referring to two independent melodic lines played simultaneously

NOTES

"common ground." The granddaughter has opened the door "for everyone" by using her unique ability to communicate across language and culture.

Hayan Charara is the author of three poetry collections and a children's book, and editor of *Inclined to Speak,* an anthology of contemporary Arab American poetry. He teaches literature and creative writing at the University of Houston.

✏ WRITE

DISCUSSION: Reading a piece of literary criticism can help a reader develop or sharpen his or her own interpretation of a piece of literature. What insights about the poem did this essay provide? How did reading this essay change or deepen your interpretation of the poem? What strategies for close reading can you learn from this essay? How will you apply these strategies in the future? Prepare for your discussion by selecting several pieces of textual evidence from the essay or the poem and by preparing original analysis to reference while sharing your ideas with your peers.

Letter from Birmingham Jail

ARGUMENTATIVE TEXT
Martin Luther King Jr.
1963

Introduction

Dr. Martin Luther King Jr. (1929–1968) was one of the leaders of the civil rights movement in America in the 1950s and '60s. "Letter from Birmingham Jail" lays out his eloquent argument for change, written in the midst of the efforts to protest Jim Crow laws and racial violence in Birmingham, Alabama. Knowing that they would be arrested, King and other members of the Alabama Christian Movement for Human Rights and the Southern Christian Leadership Conference used picketing, sit-ins, and marches to demand change. Nine days into this campaign, King was arrested alongside other prominent protesters. King's letter, written four days later in his jail cell on the margins of newspapers and on smuggled paper, responded to a newspaper article titled "A Call to Unity" in which eight white clergymen suggested that civil rights should be gained through the court system and not via protest. The letter is considered a seminal text of the Civil Rights Era.

"Oppressed people cannot remain oppressed forever."

Note: The text you are about to read contains offensive language. Remember to be mindful of the thoughts and feelings of your peers as you read and discuss this text. Please consult your teacher for additional guidance and support.

16 April 1963
My Dear Fellow Clergymen:

1   While confined here in the Birmingham city jail, I came across your recent statement calling my present activities "unwise and untimely." Seldom do I pause to answer criticism of my work and ideas. If I sought to answer all the criticisms that cross my desk, my secretaries would have little time for anything other than such correspondence in the course of the day, and I would have no time for constructive work. But since I feel that you are men of genuine good will and that your criticisms are sincerely set forth, I want to try to answer your statement in what I hope will be patient and reasonable terms.

2   I think I should indicate why I am here in Birmingham, since you have been influenced by the view which argues against "outsiders coming in." I have the honor of serving as president of the Southern Christian Leadership Conference, an organization operating in every southern state, with headquarters in Atlanta, Georgia. We have some eighty five affiliated organizations across the South, and one of them is the Alabama Christian Movement for Human Rights. Frequently we share staff, educational and financial resources with our affiliates. Several months ago the affiliate here in Birmingham asked us to be on call to engage in a nonviolent direct action program if such were deemed necessary. We readily **consented**, and when the hour came we lived up to our promise. So I, along with several members of my staff, am here because I was invited here. I am here because I have organizational ties here.

3   But more basically, I am in Birmingham because injustice is here. Just as the prophets of the eighth century B.C. left their villages and carried their "thus saith the Lord" far beyond the boundaries of their home towns, and just as the Apostle Paul left his village of Tarsus and carried the gospel of Jesus Christ to the far corners of the Greco Roman world, so am I compelled to carry the

Skill:
Primary and Secondary Sources

Here I see King referring to stories from the Bible. I know the Bible is a primary source because it is considered an original firsthand account. King's use of it makes it a secondary source for me because he is interpreting a primary source. He uses the Bible to liken the freedom movement to the spreading of the gospel in early Christianity.

gospel of freedom beyond my own home town. Like Paul, I must constantly respond to the Macedonian call for aid.

4   Moreover, I am **cognizant** of the interrelatedness of all communities and states. I cannot sit idly by in Atlanta and not be concerned about what happens in Birmingham. Injustice anywhere is a threat to justice everywhere. We are caught in an inescapable network of mutuality, tied in a single garment of destiny. Whatever affects one directly, affects all indirectly. Never again can we afford to live with the narrow, provincial "outside agitator" idea. Anyone who lives inside the United States can never be considered an outsider anywhere within its bounds.

5   You deplore the demonstrations taking place in Birmingham. But your statement, I am sorry to say, fails to express a similar concern for the conditions that brought about the demonstrations. I am sure that none of you would want to rest content with the superficial kind of social analysis that deals merely with effects and does not grapple with underlying causes. It is unfortunate that demonstrations are taking place in Birmingham, but it is even more unfortunate that the city's white power structure left the Negro community with no alternative.

6   In any nonviolent campaign there are four basic steps: collection of the facts to determine whether injustices exist; negotiation; self purification; and direct action. We have gone through all these steps in Birmingham. There can be no gainsaying the fact that racial injustice engulfs this community. Birmingham is probably the most thoroughly segregated city in the United States. Its ugly record of brutality is widely known. Negroes have experienced grossly unjust treatment in the courts. There have been more unsolved bombings of Negro homes and churches in Birmingham than in any other city in the nation. These are the hard, brutal facts of the case. On the basis of these conditions, Negro leaders sought to negotiate with the city fathers. But the latter consistently refused to engage in good faith negotiation.

7   Then, last September, came the opportunity to talk with leaders of Birmingham's economic community. In the course of the negotiations, certain promises were made by the merchants—for example, to remove the stores' humiliating racial signs. On the basis of these promises, the Reverend Fred Shuttlesworth and the leaders of the Alabama Christian Movement for Human Rights agreed to a **moratorium** on all demonstrations. As the weeks and months went by, we realized that we were the victims of a broken promise. A few signs, briefly removed, returned; the others remained.

8   As in so many past experiences, our hopes had been blasted, and the shadow of deep disappointment settled upon us. We had no alternative except to prepare for direct action, whereby we would present our very bodies as a

Skill:
Arguments and Claims

King makes the claim that injustice matters wherever it happens. He uses reasoning to support his claim, arguing that all communities are interrelated. He concludes that everyone should protest any acts of injustice in the country.

Skill:
Primary and Secondary Sources

King speaks in biblical terms to develop his concept of justice, comparing the freedom movement to the struggle of early Christians. The people in the movement lay their bodies down for their beliefs in the same way as early Christians.

means of laying our case before the conscience of the local and the national community. Mindful of the difficulties involved, we decided to undertake a process of self purification. We began a series of workshops on nonviolence, and we repeatedly asked ourselves: "Are you able to accept blows without retaliating?" "Are you able to endure the ordeal of jail?" We decided to schedule our direct action program for the Easter season, realizing that except for Christmas, this is the main shopping period of the year. Knowing that a strong economic-withdrawal program would be the by product of direct action, we felt that this would be the best time to bring pressure to bear on the merchants for the needed change.

Skill:
Rhetoric

King offers logical reasoning, showing evidence of all the times they changed the timing of protests to be thoughtful to the community. With this rhetorical device he strengthens his claim that the movement could not wait any longer.

9   Then it occurred to us that Birmingham's mayoral election was coming up in March, and we speedily decided to postpone action until after election day. When we discovered that the Commissioner of Public Safety, Eugene "Bull" Connor, had piled up enough votes to be in the run off, we decided again to postpone action until the day after the run off so that the demonstrations could not be used to cloud the issues. Like many others, we waited to see Mr. Connor[1] defeated, and to this end we endured postponement after postponement. Having aided in this community need, we felt that our direct action program could be delayed no longer.

10   You may well ask: "Why direct action? Why sit ins, marches and so forth? Isn't negotiation a better path?" You are quite right in calling for negotiation. Indeed, this is the very purpose of direct action. Nonviolent direct action seeks to create such a crisis and foster such a tension that a community which has constantly refused to negotiate is forced to confront the issue. It seeks so to dramatize the issue that it can no longer be ignored. My citing the creation of tension as part of the work of the nonviolent resister may sound rather shocking. But I must confess that I am not afraid of the word "tension." I have earnestly opposed violent tension, but there is a type of constructive, nonviolent tension which is necessary for growth. Just as Socrates felt that it was necessary to create a tension in the mind so that individuals could rise from the bondage of myths and half truths to the unfettered realm of creative analysis and objective appraisal, so must we see the need for nonviolent gadflies to create the kind of tension in society that will help men rise from the dark depths of prejudice and racism to the majestic heights of understanding and brotherhood.

11   The purpose of our direct action program is to create a situation so crisis packed that it will inevitably open the door to negotiation. I therefore concur with you in your call for negotiation. Too long has our beloved Southland been bogged down in a tragic effort to live in monologue rather than dialogue.

---

1. **Mr. Connor** Eugene "Bull" Connor, the segregationist mayoral candidate and Commissioner of Public Safety that used dogs and water hoses on black civil rights activists

12 One of the basic points in your statement is that the action that I and my associates have taken in Birmingham is untimely. Some have asked: "Why didn't you give the new city administration time to act?" The only answer that I can give to this query is that the new Birmingham administration must be prodded about as much as the outgoing one, before it will act. We are sadly mistaken if we feel that the election of Albert Boutwell as mayor will bring the millennium to Birmingham. While Mr. Boutwell is a much more gentle person than Mr. Connor, they are both segregationists, dedicated to maintenance of the **status quo**. I have hope that Mr. Boutwell will be reasonable enough to see the futility of massive resistance to desegregation. But he will not see this without pressure from devotees of civil rights. My friends, I must say to you that we have not made a single gain in civil rights without determined legal and nonviolent pressure. Lamentably, it is an historical fact that privileged groups seldom give up their privileges voluntarily. Individuals may see the moral light and voluntarily give up their unjust posture; but, as Reinhold Niebuhr has reminded us, groups tend to be more immoral than individuals.

13 We know through painful experience that freedom is never voluntarily given by the oppressor; it must be demanded by the oppressed. Frankly, I have yet to engage in a direct action campaign that was "well timed" in the view of those who have not suffered unduly from the disease of segregation. For years now I have heard the word "Wait!" It rings in the ear of every Negro with piercing familiarity. This "Wait" has almost always meant "Never." We must come to see, with one of our distinguished jurists, that "justice too long delayed is justice denied."

14 We have waited for more than 340 years for our constitutional and God given rights. The nations of Asia and Africa are moving with jetlike speed toward gaining political independence, but we still creep at horse and buggy pace toward gaining a cup of coffee at a lunch counter. Perhaps it is easy for those who have never felt the stinging darts of segregation to say, "Wait." But when you have seen vicious mobs lynch your mothers and fathers at will and drown your sisters and brothers at whim; when you have seen hate filled policemen curse, kick and even kill your black brothers and sisters; when you see the vast majority of your twenty million Negro brothers smothering in an airtight cage of poverty in the midst of an affluent society; when you suddenly find your tongue twisted and your speech stammering as you seek to explain to your six-year-old daughter why she can't go to the public amusement park that has just been advertised on television, and see tears welling up in her eyes when she is told that Funtown is closed to colored children, and see ominous clouds of inferiority beginning to form in her little mental sky, and see her beginning to distort her personality by developing an unconscious bitterness toward white people; when you have to concoct an answer for a five-year-old son who is asking: "Daddy, why do white people treat colored people so mean?"; when you take a cross-country drive and find it necessary

Skill:
Rhetoric

This passage grabbed me because it is so upsetting! The injustices that King describes here cause a strong emotional reaction. I think it would be hard for someone to not be moved by what King describes here.

to sleep night after night in the uncomfortable corners of your automobile because no motel will accept you; when you are humiliated day in and day out by nagging signs reading "white" and "colored"; when your first name becomes "n-----," your middle name becomes "boy" (however old you are) and your last name becomes "John," and your wife and mother are never given the respected title "Mrs."; when you are harried by day and haunted by night by the fact that you are a Negro, living constantly at tiptoe stance, never quite knowing what to expect next, and are plagued with inner fears and outer resentments; when you are forever fighting a degenerating sense of "nobodiness"—then you will understand why we find it difficult to wait. There comes a time when the cup of endurance runs over, and men are no longer willing to be plunged into the abyss of despair. I hope, sirs, you can understand our legitimate and unavoidable impatience.

Skill: Arguments and Claims

King uses reasoning to defend his argument that "one has a moral responsibility to disobey unjust laws." He cites the opinion of St. Augustine in his reasoning, quoting the expert opinion of someone who will appeal to his audience.

15 You express a great deal of anxiety over our willingness to break laws. This is certainly a legitimate concern. Since we so diligently urge people to obey the Supreme Court's decision of 1954[2] outlawing segregation in the public schools, at first glance it may seem rather paradoxical for us consciously to break laws. One may well ask: "How can you advocate breaking some laws and obeying others?" The answer lies in the fact that there are two types of laws: just and unjust. I would be the first to advocate obeying just laws. One has not only a legal but a moral responsibility to obey just laws. Conversely, one has a moral responsibility to disobey unjust laws. I would agree with St. Augustine that "an unjust law is no law at all."

16 Now, what is the difference between the two? How does one determine whether a law is just or unjust? A just law is a man-made code that squares with the moral law or the law of God. An unjust law is a code that is out of harmony with the moral law. To put it in the terms of St. Thomas Aquinas: An unjust law is a human law that is not rooted in eternal law and natural law. Any law that uplifts human personality is just. Any law that degrades human personality is unjust. All segregation statutes are unjust because segregation distorts the soul and damages the personality. It gives the segregator a false sense of superiority and the segregated a false sense of inferiority. Segregation, to use the terminology of the Jewish philosopher Martin Buber, substitutes an "I it" relationship for an "I thou" relationship and ends up relegating persons to the status of things. Hence segregation is not only politically, economically and sociologically unsound, it is morally wrong and sinful. Paul Tillich has said that sin is separation. Is not segregation an existential expression of man's tragic separation, his awful estrangement, his terrible sinfulness? Thus it is that I can urge men to obey the 1954 decision of the Supreme Court, for it is morally

2. **Supreme Court's decision of 1954** the landmark Supreme Court case *Brown v. Board of Education* which declared state laws that segregated schools by race to be unconstitutional

right; and I can urge them to disobey segregation ordinances, for they are morally wrong.

17　Let us consider a more concrete example of just and unjust laws. An unjust law is a code that a numerical or power majority group compels a minority group to obey but does not make binding on itself. This is difference made legal. By the same token, a just law is a code that a majority compels a minority to follow and that it is willing to follow itself. This is sameness made legal.

18　Let me give another explanation. A law is unjust if it is inflicted on a minority that, as a result of being denied the right to vote, had no part in enacting or devising the law. Who can say that the legislature of Alabama which set up that state's segregation laws was democratically elected? Throughout Alabama all sorts of devious methods are used to prevent Negroes from becoming registered voters, and there are some counties in which, even though Negroes constitute a majority of the population, not a single Negro is registered. Can any law enacted under such circumstances be considered democratically structured?

19　Sometimes a law is just on its face and unjust in its application. For instance, I have been arrested on a charge of parading without a permit. Now, there is nothing wrong in having an ordinance which requires a permit for a parade. But such an ordinance becomes unjust when it is used to maintain segregation and to deny citizens the First-Amendment privilege of peaceful assembly and protest.

20　I hope you are able to see the distinction I am trying to point out. In no sense do I advocate evading or defying the law, as would the rabid segregationist. That would lead to anarchy. One who breaks an unjust law must do so openly, lovingly, and with a willingness to accept the penalty. I submit that an individual who breaks a law that conscience tells him is unjust, and who willingly accepts the penalty of imprisonment in order to arouse the conscience of the community over its injustice, is in reality expressing the highest respect for law.

21　Of course, there is nothing new about this kind of civil disobedience. It was evidenced sublimely in the refusal of Shadrach, Meshach and Abednego to obey the laws of Nebuchadnezzar, on the ground that a higher moral law was at stake. It was practiced superbly by the early Christians, who were willing to face hungry lions and the excruciating pain of chopping blocks rather than submit to certain unjust laws of the Roman Empire. To a degree, academic freedom is a reality today because Socrates practiced civil disobedience. In our own nation, the Boston Tea Party represented a massive act of civil disobedience.

22 We should never forget that everything Adolf Hitler did in Germany was "legal" and everything the Hungarian freedom fighters did in Hungary was "illegal." It was "illegal" to aid and comfort a Jew in Hitler's Germany. Even so, I am sure that, had I lived in Germany at the time, I would have aided and comforted my Jewish brothers. If today I lived in a Communist country where certain principles dear to the Christian faith are suppressed, I would openly advocate disobeying that country's antireligious laws.

23 I must make two honest confessions to you, my Christian and Jewish brothers. First, I must confess that over the past few years I have been gravely disappointed with the white moderate. I have almost reached the regrettable conclusion that the Negro's great stumbling block in his stride toward freedom is not the White Citizen's Counciler[3] or the Ku Klux Klanner, but the white moderate, who is more devoted to "order" than to justice; who prefers a negative peace which is the absence of tension to a positive peace which is the presence of justice; who constantly says: "I agree with you in the goal you seek, but I cannot agree with your methods of direct action"; who paternalistically believes he can set the timetable for another man's freedom; who lives by a mythical concept of time and who constantly advises the Negro to wait for a "more convenient season." Shallow understanding from people of good will is more frustrating than absolute misunderstanding from people of ill will. Lukewarm acceptance is much more bewildering than outright rejection.

24 I had hoped that the white moderate would understand that law and order exist for the purpose of establishing justice and that when they fail in this purpose they become the dangerously structured dams that block the flow of social progress. I had hoped that the white moderate would understand that the present tension in the South is a necessary phase of the transition from an obnoxious negative peace, in which the Negro passively accepted his unjust plight, to a substantive and positive peace, in which all men will respect the dignity and worth of human personality. Actually, we who engage in nonviolent direct action are not the creators of tension. We merely bring to the surface the hidden tension that is already alive. We bring it out in the open, where it can be seen and dealt with. Like a boil that can never be cured so long as it is covered up but must be opened with all its ugliness to the natural medicines of air and light, injustice must be exposed, with all the tension its exposure creates, to the light of human conscience and the air of national opinion before it can be cured.

25 In your statement you assert that our actions, even though peaceful, must be condemned because they **precipitate** violence. But is this a logical assertion? Isn't this like condemning a robbed man because his possession of money

3. **White Citizen's Counciler** a member of a White Citizens Council, groups that were formed after, and in continued opposition to, the Supreme Court's desegregation of schools

precipitated the evil act of robbery? Isn't this like condemning Socrates because his unswerving commitment to truth and his philosophical inquiries precipitated the act by the misguided populace in which they made him drink hemlock[4]? Isn't this like condemning Jesus because his unique God consciousness and never ceasing devotion to God's will precipitated the evil act of crucifixion? We must come to see that, as the federal courts have consistently affirmed, it is wrong to urge an individual to cease his efforts to gain his basic constitutional rights because the quest may precipitate violence. Society must protect the robbed and punish the robber.

26   I had also hoped that the white moderate would reject the myth concerning time in relation to the struggle for freedom. I have just received a letter from a white brother in Texas. He writes: "All Christians know that the colored people will receive equal rights eventually, but it is possible that you are in too great a religious hurry. It has taken Christianity almost two thousand years to accomplish what it has. The teachings of Christ take time to come to earth." Such an attitude stems from a tragic misconception of time, from the strangely irrational notion that there is something in the very flow of time that will inevitably cure all ills. Actually, time itself is neutral; it can be used either destructively or constructively. More and more I feel that the people of ill will have used time much more effectively than have the people of good will. We will have to repent in this generation not merely for the hateful words and actions of the bad people but for the appalling silence of the good people. Human progress never rolls in on wheels of inevitability; it comes through the tireless efforts of men willing to be co workers with God, and without this hard work, time itself becomes an ally of the forces of social stagnation. We must use time creatively, in the knowledge that the time is always ripe to do right. Now is the time to make real the promise of democracy and transform our pending national elegy into a creative psalm of brotherhood. Now is the time to lift our national policy from the quicksand of racial injustice to the solid rock of human dignity.

27   You speak of our activity in Birmingham as extreme. At first I was rather disappointed that fellow clergymen would see my nonviolent efforts as those of an extremist. I began thinking about the fact that I stand in the middle of two opposing forces in the Negro community. One is a force of complacency, made up in part of Negroes who, as a result of long years of oppression, are so drained of self respect and a sense of "somebodiness" that they have adjusted to segregation; and in part of a few middle-class Negroes who, because of a degree of academic and economic security and because in some ways they profit by segregation, have become insensitive to the problems of the masses. The other force is one of bitterness and hatred, and it comes perilously close to advocating violence. It is expressed in the various

4. **hemlock** a lethal drink made from a poisonous plant of the same name

black nationalist groups that are springing up across the nation, the largest and best known being Elijah Muhammad's Muslim movement. Nourished by the Negro's frustration over the continued existence of racial discrimination, this movement is made up of people who have lost faith in America, who have absolutely repudiated Christianity, and who have concluded that the white man is an incorrigible "devil."

28   I have tried to stand between these two forces, saying that we need emulate neither the "do nothingism" of the complacent nor the hatred and despair of the black nationalist. For there is the more excellent way of love and nonviolent protest. I am grateful to God that, through the influence of the Negro church, the way of nonviolence became an integral part of our struggle.

29   If this philosophy had not emerged, by now many streets of the South would, I am convinced, be flowing with blood. And I am further convinced that if our white brothers dismiss as "rabble rousers" and "outside agitators" those of us who employ nonviolent direct action, and if they refuse to support our nonviolent efforts, millions of Negroes will, out of frustration and despair, seek solace and security in black nationalist ideologies—a development that would inevitably lead to a frightening racial nightmare.

30   Oppressed people cannot remain oppressed forever. The yearning for freedom eventually manifests itself, and that is what has happened to the American Negro. Something within has reminded him of his birthright of freedom, and something without has reminded him that it can be gained. Consciously or unconsciously, he has been caught up by the Zeitgeist[5], and with his black brothers of Africa and his brown and yellow brothers of Asia, South America and the Caribbean, the United States Negro is moving with a sense of great urgency toward the promised land of racial justice. If one recognizes this vital urge that has engulfed the Negro community, one should readily understand why public demonstrations are taking place. The Negro has many pent up resentments and latent frustrations, and he must release them. So let him march; let him make prayer pilgrimages to the city hall; let him go on freedom rides—and try to understand why he must do so. If his repressed emotions are not released in nonviolent ways, they will seek expression through violence; this is not a threat but a fact of history. So I have not said to my people: "Get rid of your discontent." Rather, I have tried to say that this normal and healthy discontent can be channeled into the creative outlet of nonviolent direct action. And now this approach is being termed extremist.

31   But though I was initially disappointed at being categorized as an extremist, as I continued to think about the matter I gradually gained a measure of satisfaction from the label. Was not Jesus an extremist for love: "Love your enemies, bless

---

5. **Zeitgeist** the spirit or climate of a specific age or culture (Origin: German)

them that curse you, do good to them that hate you, and pray for them which despitefully use you, and persecute you." Was not Amos an extremist for justice: "Let justice roll down like waters and righteousness like an ever flowing stream." Was not Paul an extremist for the Christian gospel: "I bear in my body the marks of the Lord Jesus." Was not Martin Luther an extremist: "Here I stand; I cannot do otherwise, so help me God." And John Bunyan: "I will stay in jail to the end of my days before I make a butchery of my conscience." And Abraham Lincoln: "This nation cannot survive half slave and half free." And Thomas Jefferson: "We hold these truths to be self evident, that all men are created equal . . ." So the question is not whether we will be extremists, but what kind of extremists we will be. Will we be extremists for hate or for love? Will we be extremists for the preservation of injustice or for the extension of justice? In that dramatic scene on Calvary's hill three men were crucified. We must never forget that all three were crucified for the same crime—the crime of extremism. Two were extremists for immorality, and thus fell below their environment. The other, Jesus Christ, was an extremist for love, truth and goodness, and thereby rose above his environment. Perhaps the South, the nation and the world are in dire need of creative extremists.

32   I had hoped that the white moderate would see this need. Perhaps I was too optimistic; perhaps I expected too much. I suppose I should have realized that few members of the oppressor race can understand the deep groans and passionate yearnings of the oppressed race, and still fewer have the vision to see that injustice must be rooted out by strong, persistent and determined action. I am thankful, however, that some of our white brothers in the South have grasped the meaning of this social revolution and committed themselves to it. They are still all too few in quantity, but they are big in quality. Some— such as Ralph McGill, Lillian Smith, Harry Golden, James McBride Dabbs, Ann Braden and Sarah Patton Boyle—have written about our struggle in eloquent and prophetic terms. Others have marched with us down nameless streets of the South. They have languished in filthy, roach infested jails, suffering the abuse and brutality of policemen who view them as "dirty n------lovers." Unlike so many of their moderate brothers and sisters, they have recognized the urgency of the moment and sensed the need for powerful "action" antidotes to combat the disease of segregation.

33   Let me take note of my other major disappointment. I have been so greatly disappointed with the white church and its leadership. Of course, there are some notable exceptions. I am not unmindful of the fact that each of you has taken some significant stands on this issue. I commend you, Reverend Stallings, for your Christian stand on this past Sunday, in welcoming Negroes to your worship service on a nonsegregated basis. I commend the Catholic leaders of this state for integrating Spring Hill College several years ago.

Please note that excerpts and passages in the StudySync® library and this workbook are intended as touchstones to generate interest in an author's work. The excerpts and passages do not substitute for the reading of entire texts, and StudySync® strongly recommends that students seek out and purchase the whole literary or informational work in order to experience it as the author intended. Links to online resellers are available in our digital library. In addition, complete works may be ordered through an authorized reseller by filling out and returning to StudySync® the order form enclosed in this workbook.

Reading & Writing Companion   73

34   But despite these notable exceptions, I must honestly reiterate that I have been disappointed with the church. I do not say this as one of those negative critics who can always find something wrong with the church. I say this as a minister of the gospel, who loves the church; who was nurtured in its bosom; who has been sustained by its spiritual blessings and who will remain true to it as long as the cord of life shall lengthen.

35   When I was suddenly catapulted into the leadership of the bus protest in Montgomery, Alabama, a few years ago, I felt we would be supported by the white church. I felt that the white ministers, priests and rabbis of the South would be among our strongest allies. Instead, some have been outright opponents, refusing to understand the freedom movement and misrepresenting its leaders; all too many others have been more cautious than courageous and have remained silent behind the anesthetizing security of stained glass windows.

36   In spite of my shattered dreams, I came to Birmingham with the hope that the white religious leadership of this community would see the justice of our cause and, with deep moral concern, would serve as the channel through which our just grievances could reach the power structure. I had hoped that each of you would understand. But again I have been disappointed.

37   I have heard numerous southern religious leaders admonish their worshipers to comply with a desegregation decision because it is the law, but I have longed to hear white ministers declare: "Follow this decree because integration is morally right and because the Negro is your brother." In the midst of blatant injustices inflicted upon the Negro, I have watched white churchmen stand on the sideline and mouth pious irrelevancies and sanctimonious trivialities. In the midst of a mighty struggle to rid our nation of racial and economic injustice, I have heard many ministers say: "Those are social issues, with which the gospel has no real concern." And I have watched many churches commit themselves to a completely other worldly religion which makes a strange, un-Biblical distinction between body and soul, between the sacred and the secular.

38   I have traveled the length and breadth of Alabama, Mississippi and all the other southern states. On sweltering summer days and crisp autumn mornings I have looked at the South's beautiful churches with their lofty spires pointing heavenward. I have beheld the impressive outlines of her massive religious education buildings. Over and over I have found myself asking: "What kind of people worship here? Who is their God? Where were their voices when the lips of Governor Barnett dripped with words of interposition and nullification? Where were they when Governor Wallace gave a clarion call for defiance and hatred? Where were their voices of support when bruised and weary Negro men and women decided to rise from the dark dungeons of complacency to the bright hills of creative protest?"

39   Yes, these questions are still in my mind. In deep disappointment I have wept over the laxity of the church. But be assured that my tears have been tears of love. There can be no deep disappointment where there is not deep love. Yes, I love the church. How could I do otherwise? I am in the rather unique position of being the son, the grandson and the great grandson of preachers. Yes, I see the church as the body of Christ. But, oh! How we have blemished and scarred that body through social neglect and through fear of being nonconformists.

40   There was a time when the church was very powerful—in the time when the early Christians rejoiced at being deemed worthy to suffer for what they believed. In those days the church was not merely a thermometer that recorded the ideas and principles of popular opinion; it was a thermostat that transformed the mores of society. Whenever the early Christians entered a town, the people in power became disturbed and immediately sought to convict the Christians for being "disturbers of the peace" and "outside agitators.'" But the Christians pressed on, in the conviction that they were "a colony of heaven," called to obey God rather than man. Small in number, they were big in commitment. They were too God-intoxicated to be "astronomically intimidated." By their effort and example they brought an end to such ancient evils as infanticide and gladiatorial contests. Things are different now. So often the contemporary church is a weak, ineffectual voice with an uncertain sound. So often it is an archdefender of the status quo. Far from being disturbed by the presence of the church, the power structure of the average community is consoled by the church's silent—and often even vocal—**sanction** of things as they are.

41   But the judgment of God is upon the church as never before. If today's church does not recapture the sacrificial spirit of the early church, it will lose its authenticity, forfeit the loyalty of millions, and be dismissed as an irrelevant social club with no meaning for the twentieth century. Every day I meet young people whose disappointment with the church has turned into outright disgust.

42   Perhaps I have once again been too optimistic. Is organized religion too inextricably bound to the status quo to save our nation and the world? Perhaps I must turn my faith to the inner spiritual church, the church within the church, as the true *ecclesia* and the hope of the world. But again I am thankful to God that some noble souls from the ranks of organized religion have broken loose from the paralyzing chains of conformity and joined us as active partners in the struggle for freedom. They have left their secure congregations and walked the streets of Albany, Georgia, with us. They have gone down the highways of the South on tortuous rides for freedom. Yes, they have gone to jail with us. Some have been dismissed from their churches, have lost the support of their bishops and fellow ministers. But they have acted in the faith that right defeated is stronger than evil triumphant. Their witness has been the spiritual salt that has preserved the true meaning of the gospel in these troubled times. They have carved a tunnel of hope through the dark mountain of disappointment.

NOTES

43   I hope the church as a whole will meet the challenge of this decisive hour. But even if the church does not come to the aid of justice, I have no despair about the future. I have no fear about the outcome of our struggle in Birmingham, even if our motives are at present misunderstood. We will reach the goal of freedom in Birmingham and all over the nation, because the goal of America is freedom. Abused and scorned though we may be, our destiny is tied up with America's destiny. Before the pilgrims landed at Plymouth, we were here. Before the pen of Jefferson etched the majestic words of the Declaration of Independence across the pages of history, we were here. For more than two centuries our forebears labored in this country without wages; they made cotton king; they built the homes of their masters while suffering gross injustice and shameful humiliation—and yet out of a bottomless vitality they continued to thrive and develop. If the inexpressible cruelties of slavery could not stop us, the opposition we now face will surely fail. We will win our freedom because the sacred heritage of our nation and the eternal will of God are embodied in our echoing demands.

44   Before closing I feel impelled to mention one other point in your statement that has troubled me profoundly. You warmly commended the Birmingham police force for keeping "order" and "preventing violence." I doubt that you would have so warmly commended the police force if you had seen its dogs sinking their teeth into unarmed, nonviolent Negroes. I doubt that you would so quickly commend the policemen if you were to observe their ugly and inhumane treatment of Negroes here in the city jail; if you were to watch them push and curse old Negro women and young Negro girls; if you were to see them slap and kick old Negro men and young boys; if you were to observe them, as they did on two occasions, refuse to give us food because we wanted to sing our grace together. I cannot join you in your praise of the Birmingham police department.

45   It is true that the police have exercised a degree of **discipline** in handling the demonstrators. In this sense they have conducted themselves rather "nonviolently" in public. But for what purpose? To preserve the evil system of segregation. Over the past few years I have consistently preached that nonviolence demands that the means we use must be as pure as the ends we seek. I have tried to make clear that it is wrong to use immoral means to attain moral ends. But now I must affirm that it is just as wrong, or perhaps even more so, to use moral means to preserve immoral ends. Perhaps Mr. Connor and his policemen have been rather nonviolent in public, as was Chief Pritchett in Albany, Georgia, but they have used the moral means of nonviolence to maintain the immoral end of racial injustice. As T. S. Eliot has said: "The last temptation is the greatest treason: To do the right deed for the wrong reason."

46   I wish you had commended the Negro sit inners and demonstrators of Birmingham for their sublime courage, their willingness to suffer and their

amazing discipline in the midst of great provocation. One day the South will recognize its real heroes. They will be the James Merediths, with the noble sense of purpose that enables them to face jeering and hostile mobs, and with the agonizing loneliness that characterizes the life of the pioneer. They will be old, oppressed, battered Negro women, symbolized in a seventy-two-year-old woman in Montgomery, Alabama, who rose up with a sense of dignity and with her people decided not to ride segregated buses, and who responded with ungrammatical profundity to one who inquired about her weariness: "My feets is tired, but my soul is at rest." They will be the young high school and college students, the young ministers of the gospel and a host of their elders, courageously and nonviolently sitting in at lunch counters and willingly going to jail for conscience' sake. One day the South will know that when these disinherited children of God sat down at lunch counters, they were in reality standing up for what is best in the American dream and for the most sacred values in our Judeo-Christian heritage, thereby bringing our nation back to those great wells of democracy which were dug deep by the founding fathers in their formulation of the Constitution and the Declaration of Independence.

47 Never before have I written so long a letter. I'm afraid it is much too long to take your precious time. I can assure you that it would have been much shorter if I had been writing from a comfortable desk, but what else can one do when he is alone in a narrow jail cell, other than write long letters, think long thoughts and pray long prayers?

48 If I have said anything in this letter that overstates the truth and indicates an unreasonable impatience, I beg you to forgive me. If I have said anything that understates the truth and indicates my having a patience that allows me to settle for anything less than brotherhood, I beg God to forgive me.

49 I hope this letter finds you strong in the faith. I also hope that circumstances will soon make it possible for me to meet each of you, not as an integrationist or a civil-rights leader but as a fellow clergyman and a Christian brother. Let us all hope that the dark clouds of racial prejudice will soon pass away and the deep fog of misunderstanding will be lifted from our fear drenched communities, and in some not too distant tomorrow the radiant stars of love and brotherhood will shine over our great nation with all their scintillating beauty.

Yours for the cause of Peace and Brotherhood,

Martin Luther King, Jr.

LETTER FROM
BIRMINGHAM JAIL

First Read

Read "Letter from Birmingham Jail." After you read, complete the Think Questions below.

☁ THINK QUESTIONS

1. According to Dr. King, why is he in Birmingham? List at least three reasons, using evidence from the text to support your response.

2. What does Dr. King mean when he says, "Injustice anywhere is a threat to justice everywhere?" What examples does he give of this concept? Include evidence from paragraphs 5–7 in your response.

3. According to Dr. King, what is the goal of direct nonviolent action?

4. Keeping in mind that the Latin root *cog* means "to learn," use context to determine the definition of the adjective **cognizant**. Once you are finished, use a print or an online dictionary to confirm the definition.

5. Use context to determine the meaning of the Latin phrase **status quo**. Then write your definition here, explaining how you determined its meaning.

Skill:
Primary and Secondary Sources

Use the Checklist to analyze Primary and Secondary Sources in "Letter from Birmingham Jail." Refer to the sample student annotations about Primary and Secondary Sources in the text.

••• CHECKLIST FOR PRIMARY AND SECONDARY SOURCES

In order to analyze and differentiate between primary and secondary sources, do the following:

✓ examine the source, noting the title, author, and date of publication, if applicable

✓ identify the genre of the source

- examples of primary sources include letters, diaries, journals, speeches, eyewitness interviews, oral histories, memoirs, and autobiographies
- examples of secondary sources include encyclopedia articles, newspaper and magazine articles, biographies, documentary films, history books, and textbooks

If the source meets one or more of the following criteria, it is considered a primary source:

✓ original, firsthand account of an event or time period

✓ writing that takes place during the event or time period

If the source meets one or more of the following criteria, it is considered a secondary source:

✓ a book or an article that analyzes and interprets primary sources

✓ a secondhand account of an historical event

✓ a book or an article that interprets or analyzes creative work

To analyze a primary or secondary source, including how it addresses themes and concepts in a text, ask the following questions:

✓ Is the source reliable and credible in its presentation of information? How do I know?

✓ How does the source address themes and concepts, such as patriotism?

✓ What gives this source historical or literary significance?

Skill:
Primary and Secondary Sources

Reread paragraph 10 of "Letter from Birmingham Jail." Then, using the Checklist on the previous page, answer the multiple-choice questions below.

⟳ YOUR TURN

1. What primary source does King use to support his argument?

    ○ A. The questions that the readers might ask
    ○ B. Socrates' views on tension
    ○ C. King's views on tension
    ○ D. The fact that the community has refused to negotiate

2. For readers of King's letter, is the above reference a primary or secondary source?

    ○ A. It's a secondary source because King is referencing a primary source.
    ○ B. It's a primary source because King is referencing a historical figure.
    ○ C. It's a secondary source because King is referencing a secondary source.
    ○ D. It's a primary source because King, the author, is a historical figure.

3. How does King's reference to a primary source contribute to making his letter a document of literary and historical significance?

    ○ A. By referencing a primary source, King is stating a new and unique idea.
    ○ B. By referencing Socrates, King is debating one of the greatest minds in history.
    ○ C. King builds on a powerful theme originally stated by Socrates, an important thinker.
    ○ D. King is helping to convince people of Socrates' argument.

Skill:
Arguments and Claims

Use the Checklist to analyze Arguments and Claims in "Letter from Birmingham Jail." Refer to the sample student annotations about Arguments and Claims in the text.

••• CHECKLIST FOR ARGUMENTS AND CLAIMS

In order to identify a speaker's or author's argument and claims, note the following:

- ✓ clues that reveal the author's opinion in the title, opening remarks or introductory paragraph, or concluding statement or paragraph

- ✓ the specific situation or circumstances about which the author is writing

- ✓ declarative statements that come before or follow a speaker's anecdote, story, or example

To delineate an author's argument and specific claims, do the following:

- ✓ note the information that the author introduces in sequential order

- ✓ note how the author structures his or her writing (claim, evidence, and conclusion)

- ✓ describe the author's argument in your own words

To analyze and evaluate the argument and specific claims, consider the following questions:

- ✓ Does the author support each claim with reasoning and evidence?

- ✓ Is the reasoning sound and the evidence sufficient?

- ✓ Do the author's claims work together to support the his or her overall argument?

- ✓ Which claims are not supported, if any?

Please note that excerpts and passages in the StudySync® library and this workbook are intended as touchstones to generate interest in an author's work. The excerpts and passages do not substitute for the reading of entire texts, and StudySync® strongly recommends that students seek out and purchase the whole literary or informational work in order to experience it as the author intended. Links to online resellers are available in our digital library. In addition, complete works may be ordered through an authorized reseller by filling out and returning to StudySync® the order form enclosed in this workbook.

Reading & Writing Companion   81

Skill:
Arguments and Claims

Reread paragraphs 30 and 31 of "Letter from Birmingham Jail." Then, using the Checklist on the previous page, answer the multiple-choice questions below.

⟳ YOUR TURN

1. This question has two parts. First, answer Part A. Then, answer Part B.

   Part A: Which claim does King make most clearly in paragraph 30?

   ○ A. When people are oppressed there will always come a time when they inevitably fight for their freedom.
   ○ B. Germans began the freedom movement.
   ○ C. People of Africa, Asia, South America, and the Caribbean are all fighting together for freedom.
   ○ D. Violence is inevitable and only a matter of time.

   Part B: Which of the following details BEST provides reason to support the claim in Part A?

   ○ A. "one should readily understand why public demonstrations are taking place"
   ○ B. "let him make prayer pilgrimages to the city hall"
   ○ C. "The Negro has many pent up resentments and latent frustrations, and he must release them."
   ○ D. "he has been caught up by the Zeitgeist"

2. This question has two parts. First, answer Part A. Then, answer Part B.

   Part A: Which claim does King make most clearly in paragraph 31?

   ○ A. Jesus would have also been condemned by the church.
   ○ B. Extremism is always right.
   ○ C. King is refuting the idea that he is an extremist.
   ○ D. Extremism is a good thing for virtuous causes.

   Part B: Based on your answer in Part A, how does King defend his claim?

   ○ A. King defends his claim with facts about the Civil War.
   ○ B. King defends his claim with expert opinions about historical figures.
   ○ C. King defends his claim by reasoning that everyone should be like historical figures.
   ○ D. King defends his claim by reasoning that many revered historical figures were extremists.

Skill:
Rhetoric

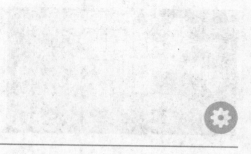

Use the Checklist to analyze Rhetoric in "Letter from Birmingham Jail." Refer to the sample student annotations about Rhetoric in the text.

••• CHECKLIST FOR RHETORIC

In order to determine an author's point of view or purpose in a text and analyze how an author uses rhetoric, note the following:

✓ Rhetoric refers to the persuasive use of language in a text or speech, and authors or speakers may use different rhetorical devices to advance a purpose or a specific point of view:

- logical reasoning, supported by evidence, facts, or statistics
- an emotional plea by personalizing a situation or occurrence
- reminding readers or listeners of their shared values and beliefs

✓ An author or speaker may be objective or biased, and the use of rhetoric may communicate his or her point of view, or attitude toward a topic, to readers.

To analyze how an author or speaker uses rhetoric, consider the following questions:

✓ Does the author or speaker employ rhetoric in the text? If so, what kind?

✓ How does the author or speaker try to persuade readers? Are there any emotional pleas meant to evoke sympathy, or does the author only present facts and statistics?

✓ How does the author's or speaker's use of rhetoric reveal his or her purpose for writing?

✓ What does the use of rhetoric disclose about the author's or speaker's point of view toward the subject?

Please note that excerpts and passages in the StudySync® library and this workbook are intended as touchstones to generate interest in an author's work. The excerpts and passages do not substitute for the reading of entire texts, and StudySync® strongly recommends that students seek out and purchase the whole literary or informational work in order to experience it as the author intended. Links to online resellers are available in our digital library. In addition, complete works may be ordered through an authorized reseller by filling out and returning to StudySync® the order form enclosed in this workbook.

Reading & Writing Companion   83

Skill:
Rhetoric

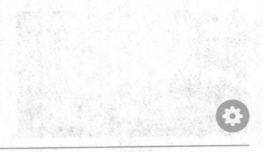

Reread paragraphs 44–46 of "Letter from Birmingham Jail." Then, using the Checklist on the previous page, answer the multiple-choice questions below.

⟳ YOUR TURN

1. Identify the effect of the logical reasoning that King employs in paragraph 44.

   ○ A. It refutes the idea that the Birmingham police have been keeping "order" and "preventing violence."
   ○ B. It shows King's disappointment in the clergymen who think that the Birmingham police have been peaceful.
   ○ C. It explains why the actions of the Birmingham police are inherently wrong.
   ○ D. It is used to explain why the actions of the protestors are just.

2. What does King's emotional appeal in paragraph 46 accomplish?

   ○ A. It contrasts the protesters in Birmingham with protesters in other Southern cities.
   ○ B. It highlights the positive traits of the people who are protesting for greater freedoms.
   ○ C. It clarifies the idea that there are various ways to protest injustice.
   ○ D. It emphasizes the moral evil of the people who oppose extending civil rights to all.

3. Why does King refer to the American dream and sacred Judeo-Christian values at the end of paragraph 46?

   ○ A. It explains how the protestors are seen in the South.
   ○ B. It describes why the clergymen are wrong.
   ○ C. It highlights the shared values between the protestors and the clergymen.
   ○ D. It highlights the courage and resolve of those participating in the protest movement.

LETTER FROM
BIRMINGHAM JAIL

Close Read

Reread "Letter from Birmingham Jail." As you reread, complete the Skills Focus questions below. Then use your answers and annotations from the questions to help you complete the Write activity.

◎ SKILLS FOCUS

1. In paragraph 15, identify two examples of primary sources cited by Dr. King. Explain how each source helps him reinforce his argument.

2. Identify the claim that Dr. Martin Luther King Jr. makes in paragraph 21. Explain how his use of an appeal supports that claim.

3. Identify the rhetorical device and the type of appeal that King uses in paragraph 26. Explain how they are intended to affect the reader.

4. Explain the rhetorical shift in paragraphs 38–39. Explain the purpose of this device in King's argument.

5. Identify the conclusion of King's letter. Describe the appeal King uses to help create a convincing conclusion to his argument and make his words matter.

✏ WRITE

RHETORICAL ANALYSIS: One reason that "Letter from Birmingham Jail" remains one of the best-known texts of the civil rights era is because of the powerful rhetoric that Dr. Martin Luther King Jr. uses to advocate for nonviolent resistance to racism. Write a response in which you delineate and evaluate King's argument, his specific claims, his rhetorical appeals, his use of sources, and his argument's conclusion. Support your analysis with evidence from the text.

Please note that excerpts and passages in the StudySync® library and this workbook are intended as touchstones to generate interest in an author's work. The excerpts and passages do not substitute for the reading of entire texts, and StudySync® strongly recommends that students seek out and purchase the whole literary or informational work in order to experience it as the author intended. Links to online resellers are available in our digital library. In addition, complete works may be ordered through an authorized reseller by filling out and returning to StudySync® the order form enclosed in this workbook.

Reading & Writing
Companion   **85**

A Voice

POETRY
Pat Mora
1979

Introduction

Author Pat Mora (b. 1942) grew up along the border between the United States and Mexico, and her writing contains great insight into the diverse perspectives of the region. In ten moving stanzas, the speaker of "A Voice" tells the story of how her mother learned a new language and assimilated into American culture—and the impact her mother's experiences have had on her own life. On the border between two markedly different countries, her mother's displacement is felt both culturally and physically, among her family and loved ones, as well as in her own heart.

"'How did I do it?' you ask me now."

NOTES

1   Even the lights on the stage **unrelenting**
2   as the desert sun couldn't hide the other
3   students, their eyes also unrelenting,
4   students who spoke English every night

5   as they ate their meat, potatoes, gravy.
6   Not you. In your house that smelled like
7   rose powder, you spoke Spanish formal
8   as your father, the **judge** without a courtroom

9   in the country he floated to in the dark
10   on a flatbed truck. He walked slow
11   as a hot river down the narrow hall
12   of your house. You never dared to race past him,

13   to say, "Please move," in the language
14   you learned effortlessly, as you learned to run,
15   the language forbidden at home, though your mother
16   said you learned it to fight with the neighbors.

17   You liked winning with words. You liked
18   writing speeches about **patriotism** and **democracy**.
19   You liked all the faces looking at you, all those eyes.
20   "How did I do it?" you ask me now. "How did I do it

21   when my parents didn't understand?"
22   The family story says your voice is the voice
23   of an aunt in Mexico, spunky as a peacock.
24   Family stories sing of what lives in the blood.

25   You told me only once about the time you went
26   to the state capitol, your family proud as if
27   you'd been named governor. But when you looked
28   around, the only Mexican in the auditorium,

NOTES

29   you wanted to hide from those strange faces.
30   Their eyes were pinpricks, and you faked
31   hoarseness. You, who are never at a loss
32   for words, felt your breath stick in your throat

33   like an ice-cube. "I can't," you whispered.
34   "I can't." Yet you did. Not that day but years later.
35   You taught the four of us to speak up.
36   This is America, Mom. The undo-able is done

37   in the next **generation**. Your breath moves
38   through the family like the wind
39   moves through the trees.

"A Voice" is reprinted with permission from the publisher of "My Own True Name" by Pat Mora (© 2000 Arte Público Press - University of Houston)

✏ WRITE

LITERARY ANALYSIS: In "A Voice," the speaker shares her fear of how others might perceive her at a speech contest due to her background. How does the speaker's characterization of her mother convey her attitude toward her background?

Speech to the
Second Virginia
Convention

ARGUMENTATIVE TEXT
Patrick Henry
1775

Introduction

Patrick Henry (1736–1799) was an orator, attorney, twice governor of Virginia and one of the Founding Fathers of the United States. Given on the eve of America's Revolutionary War, Patrick Henry's "Speech to the Second Virginia Convention" articulated his radical views with carefully constructed language and emotional appeals. Hoping to convince Virginia's House of Burgesses to pass a resolution of independence against Britain and to provide military support for the cause, Henry appealed to the patriotism of those in attendance—including George Washington, Thomas Jefferson, and many more. Today, Henry is best remembered for his famous call-to-arms, "Give me liberty or give me death!"

"I know not what course others may take; but as for me, give me liberty or give me death!"

Skill:
Author's Purpose
and Point of View

Henry makes a point of being respectful, even though it's clear he's going to say things that others don't agree with. To show how serious this is, Henry makes the point that this a question of freedom vs. slavery.

1   Mr. President, no man thinks more highly than I do of the patriotism, as well as abilities, of the very worthy gentlemen who have just **addressed** the House. But different men often see the same subject in different lights; and, therefore, I hope it will not be thought disrespectful to those gentlemen if, entertaining as I do, opinions of a character very opposite to theirs, I shall speak forth my sentiments freely, and without reserve. This is no time for ceremony. The question before the House is one of awful moment to this country. For my own part, I consider it as nothing less than a question of freedom or slavery; and in **proportion** to the magnitude of the subject ought to be the freedom of the debate. It is only in this way that we can hope to arrive at truth, and fulfill the great responsibility which we hold to God and our country. Should I keep back my opinions at such a time, through fear of giving offence, I should consider myself as guilty of treason towards my country, and of an act of disloyalty toward the majesty of heaven, which I revere above all earthly kings.

2   Mr. President, it is natural to man to indulge in the illusions of hope. We are apt to shut our eyes against a painful truth, and listen to the song of that siren[1] till she transforms us into beasts. Is this the part of wise men, engaged in a great and arduous struggle for liberty? Are we **disposed** to be of the number of those who, having eyes, see not, and, having ears, hear not, the things which so nearly concern their temporal salvation? For my part, whatever anguish of spirit it may cost, I am willing to know the whole truth; to know the worst, and to provide for it.

Give me liberty, or give me death!, lithograph (1876) from the Library of Congress

---

1. **the song of that siren** a reference to the Sirens of Greek Mythology, who sang so beautifully that men were mesmerized and led to their ends

3   I have but one lamp by which my feet are guided; and that is the lamp of experience. I know of no way of judging of the future but by the past. And judging by the past, I wish to know what there has been in the conduct of the British ministry for the last ten years, to justify those hopes with which gentlemen have been pleased to solace themselves, and the House? Is it that insidious smile with which our petition has been lately received[2]? Trust it not, sir; it will prove a snare to your feet. Suffer not yourselves to be betrayed with a kiss. Ask yourselves how this gracious reception of our petition comports with these war-like preparations which cover our waters and darken our land. Are fleets and armies necessary to a work of love and reconciliation? Have we shown ourselves so unwilling to be reconciled, that force must be called in to win back our love? Let us not deceive ourselves, sir. These are the implements of war and **subjugation**; the last arguments to which kings resort. I ask, gentlemen, sir, what means this martial array, if its purpose be not to force us to submission? Can gentlemen assign any other possible motive for it?

4   Has Great Britain any enemy, in this quarter of the world, to call for all this accumulation of navies and armies? No, sir, she has none. They are meant for us; they can be meant for no other. They are sent over to bind and rivet upon us those chains which the British ministry have been so long forging. And what have we to oppose to them? Shall we try argument? Sir, we have been trying that for the last ten years. Have we anything new to offer upon the subject? Nothing. We have held the subject up in every light of which it is capable; but it has been all in vain. Shall we resort to entreaty and humble supplication? What terms shall we find which have not been already exhausted? Let us not, I beseech you, sir, deceive ourselves. Sir, we have done everything that could be done, to avert the storm which is now coming on. We have petitioned; we have remonstrated; we have supplicated; we have prostrated ourselves before the throne, and have implored its interposition to arrest the tyrannical hands of the ministry and Parliament. Our petitions have been slighted; our remonstrances have produced additional violence and insult; our supplications have been disregarded; and we have been spurned, with contempt, from the foot of the throne. In vain, after these things, may we indulge the fond hope of peace and reconciliation. There is no longer any room for hope. If we wish to be free, if we mean to preserve inviolate those inestimable privileges for which we have been so long contending, if we mean not basely to abandon the noble struggle in which we have been so long engaged, and which we have pledged ourselves never to abandon until the glorious object of our contest shall be obtained, we must fight! I repeat it, sir, we must fight! An appeal to arms and to the God of Hosts is all that is left us!

Skill:
Author's Purpose
and Point of View

Henry tries to persuade the House that the only option is for the colonists to fight if they truly want freedom from British rule. He uses powerful rhetoric and repeated phrases to lead up to his forceful three-word message at the end.

2. **Is it that insidious smile with which our petition has lately been received** the "petition" here being a protest by the First Continental Congress against new tax laws

Skill:
Language, Style,
and Audience

Patrick Henry's continued questions emphasize his message that the time for action has come. He carefully chooses phrases such as "holy cause of liberty" and "invincible" to persuade his audience that the colonists' cause is just.

5   They tell us, sir, that we are weak; unable to cope with so **formidable** an adversary. But when shall we be stronger? Will it be the next week, or the next year? Will it be when we are totally disarmed, and when a British guard shall be stationed in every house? Shall we gather strength by irresolution and inaction? Shall we acquire the means of effectual resistance, by lying supinely on our backs, and hugging the delusive phantom of hope, until our enemies shall have bound us hand and foot? Sir, we are not weak if we make a proper use of those means which the God of nature hath placed in our power. Three millions of people, armed in the holy cause of liberty, and in such a country as that which we possess, are invincible by any force which our enemy can send against us. Besides, sir, we shall not fight our battles alone. There is a just God who presides over the destinies of nations; and who will raise up friends to fight our battles for us. The battle, sir, is not to the strong alone; it is to the vigilant, the active, the brave. Besides, sir, we have no election. If we were base enough to desire it, it is now too late to retire from the contest. There is no retreat but in submission and slavery! Our chains are forged! Their clanking may be heard on the plains of Boston! The war is inevitable and let it come! I repeat it, sir, let it come. It is in vain, sir, to extenuate the matter. Gentlemen may cry, Peace, Peace but there is no peace. The war is actually begun! The next gale that sweeps from the north will bring to our ears the clash of resounding arms! Our brethren are already in the field! Why stand we here idle? What is it that gentlemen wish? What would they have? Is life so dear, or peace so sweet, as to be purchased at the price of chains and slavery? Forbid it, Almighty God! I know not what course others may take; but as for me, give me liberty or give me death!

First Read

Read "Speech to the Second Virginia Convention." After you read, complete the Think Questions below.

 THINK QUESTIONS

1. Who is Patrick Henry's audience for this speech, and what is the occasion or historical situation in which he is giving the speech? Support your answer with evidence from the text.

2. According to paragraph 4, what efforts have the American colonists already made to negotiate with Britain? Were those efforts successful? Support your answer with evidence from the text.

3. Henry claims that the British view the Americans as "weak." How does he respond to this criticism? Use evidence from paragraph 5 to support your response.

4. The Latin prefix *sub-* means "under," and the Latin word *jugus* means "yoke." With this information in mind and using context clues from the text, write your best definition of the word **subjugation** here.

5. Use context clues to determine the meaning of the word **formidable** as it is used in the speech. Write your definition of *formidable* here and explain how you figured it out.

Please note that excerpts and passages in the StudySync® library and this workbook are intended as touchstones to generate interest in an author's work. The excerpts and passages do not substitute for the reading of entire texts, and StudySync® strongly recommends that students seek out and purchase the whole literary or informational work in order to experience it as the author intended. Links to online resellers are available in our digital library. In addition, complete works may be ordered through an authorized reseller by filling out and returning to StudySync® the order form enclosed in this workbook.

Reading & Writing Companion   **93**

AUTHOR'S PURPOSE AND POINT OF VIEW

Skill: Author's Purpose and Point of View

Use the Checklist to analyze Author's Purpose and Point of View in "Speech to the Second Virginia Convention." Refer to the sample student annotations about Author's Purpose and Point of View in the text.

••• CHECKLIST FOR AUTHOR'S PURPOSE AND POINT OF VIEW

In order to identify the author's or speaker's purpose and point of view, do the following:

✓ Note the evidence that the author or speaker offers to support his or her point of view.

✓ Clarify if the author or speaker includes any fallacious reasoning or errors in logic that invalidate or overturn an argument, such as drawing a conclusion based on information that is inconclusive or questionable.

✓ Determine whether the author or speaker offers distorted or exaggerated evidence to support a point of view.

✓ Examine whether the author or speaker uses figurative language or other descriptive words in order to intensify an emotion.

✓ Identify the author's use of rhetoric, or the art of speaking and writing persuasively, such as using repetition to drive home a point.

To evaluate the author's or speaker's purpose and point of view, consider the following questions:

✓ How does the author or speaker convey, or communicate, information in the text?

✓ Does the author or speaker use figurative or emotional language? What effect does it have on the author's point of view?

✓ Are charts, graphs, maps, and other graphic aids referred to or included in the text?

✓ How does the author use rhetoric to try and persuade readers or the audience to accept a specific point of view or opinion? Is the use of rhetoric successful? Why or why not?

Skill: Author's Purpose and Point of View

Reread paragraph 2 of "Speech to the Second Virginia Convention." Then, using the Checklist on the previous page, answer the multiple-choice questions below.

↻ YOUR TURN

1. What is Henry's purpose of starting this paragraph with "Mr. President"?

   ○ A. Henry knows the president is the only one in the audience he needs to convince.
   ○ B. Henry shows he has has given up on his attempt to persuade his audience.
   ○ C. Henry separates himself and the president from the rest of the audience he is addressing.
   ○ D. Henry shows respect for the audience and its leader in order to gain their respect and attention.

2. Which of the following quotes in this paragraph best achieves Henry's purpose to persuade the audience to join him in his fight for American independence?

   ○ A. "Mr. President, it is natural to man to indulge in the illusions of hope."
   ○ B. "Is this the part of wise men, engaged in a great and arduous struggle for liberty?"
   ○ C. "For my part, whatever anguish of spirit it may cost, I am willing to know the whole truth; to know the worst, and to provide for it."
   ○ D. "We are apt to shut our eyes against a painful truth, and listen to the song of that siren till she transforms us into beasts."

3. Which of the following best states Henry's point of view in this paragraph?

   ○ A. Give the British a second chance in the hope that their behavior will improve.
   ○ B. Do whatever can possibly be done to avoid the outbreak of war.
   ○ C. Face the painful truth of the current situation and prepare to respond to it.
   ○ D. Accept the current situation but plan to revisit the issue in the future.

Skill:
Language, Style, and Audience

Use the Checklist to analyze Language, Style, and Audience in "Speech to the Second Virginia Convention." Refer to the sample student annotations about Language, Style, and Audience in the text.

••• CHECKLIST FOR LANGUAGE, STYLE, AND AUDIENCE

In order to determine an author's style, do the following:

- ✓ Identify and define any unfamiliar words or phrases.

- ✓ Analyze the surrounding words and phrases as well as the context in which the specific words are being used.

- ✓ Note the audience—both intended and unintended—and possible reactions to the author's word choice and style.

- ✓ Examine your reaction to the author's word choice and how the author's choice affected your reaction.

In order to analyze the cumulative impact of word choice on meaning and tone, ask the following questions:

- ✓ How did your understanding of the writer's language change during your analysis?

- ✓ How does the writer's cumulative word choice impact or create meaning in the text?

- ✓ How does the writer's cumulative word choice impact or create a specific tone in the text?

- ✓ What images, feelings, or ideas do the writer's cumulative word choices evoke?

- ✓ How could various audiences interpret this language? What different possible emotional responses can you list?

Skill:
Language, Style, and Audience

Reread paragraph 5 of "Speech to the Second Virginia Convention." Then, using the Checklist on the previous page, answer the multiple-choice questions below.

⟳ YOUR TURN

1. Think about the metaphor of chains ("Our chains are forged!"). What is the most likely purpose of that metaphor?

   ○ A. The metaphor is intended to frighten the colonists into submission to Britain.
   ○ B. The metaphor reminds colonists of the harsh way in which the British punish criminals.
   ○ C. The metaphor is intended to warn colonists about the danger of going to war with Britain.
   ○ D. The metaphor reinforces the idea that the British will not grant freedom to the colonists.

2. Near the end of the paragraph, Patrick Henry phrases his thoughts in the form of questions and exclamations. What purpose does that language serve?

   ○ A. The language expresses Henry's anger over the past actions of the British.
   ○ B. The language captures Henry's passion and his belief that now is the time for action.
   ○ C. The language encourages Henry's audience to seek God's help in the coming war.
   ○ D. The language begs Henry's audience to prepare to protect themselves and their families.

Skill:
Compare and Contrast

Use the Checklist to analyze Compare and Contrast in "Speech to the Second Virginia Convention."

••• CHECKLIST FOR COMPARE AND CONTRAST

In order to compare and contrast informational texts, including seminal U.S. documents of historical and literary significance, do the following:

✓ Choose two or more seminal, groundbreaking, or influential documents of literary and historical significance, such as Franklin Roosevelt's Four Freedoms Speech or Martin Luther King, Jr.'s "Letter from Birmingham Jail."

✓ Identify the main idea in each document and the themes and concepts outlined in each text.

✓ Compare and contrast two or more of these documents and note the similarities and differences between them, including how they address related themes and concepts.

To analyze seminal U.S. documents, including how they address related themes and concepts, consider the following questions:

✓ Are the texts I have chosen considered to be seminal U.S. documents of both historical and literary significance?

✓ What themes or concepts are apparent in each of these documents?

✓ Have I determined the main idea in each document? What details support it?

✓ How are the ideas, themes, and concepts in these documents similar and different?

Skill:
Compare and Contrast

Reread paragraph 24 of King's "Letter from Birmingham Jail" and paragraph 5 of Henry's "Speech to the Second Virginia Convention." Then, using the Checklist on the previous page, answer the multiple-choice questions below.

⟳ YOUR TURN

1. Which of the following best summarizes the central ideas of King's letter and Henry's speech and how they are related?

   ○ A. King and Henry both are calling to fight for the freedom of oppression in the U.S. using whatever means necessary.

   ○ B. King is advocating for the acceptance of the status quo in the U.S. while Henry is is not, although both of them are addressing themes of oppression in seminal fictional texts.

   ○ C. In seminal U.S. historical documents, King and Henry are both speaking directly to their opponents to advocate further action to end oppression.

   ○ D. Henry thinks the only way to make change in America is with violence while King hopes to make change using words, so the documents are not related.

2. Which of the following statements regarding literary devices in each historical document is true?

   ○ A. King uses metaphors and similes to strengthen his argument, while Henry speaks in plain language.

   ○ B. King uses metaphors and similes to strengthen his argument, while Henry uses questioning and hyperbole to strengthen his speech.

   ○ C. Neither Henry nor King use literary devices but instead use factual statements only.

   ○ D. Henry's speech is a metaphor for slavery, whereas King uses similes to describe the civil rights era.

Close Read

Reread "Speech to the Second Virginia Convention." As you reread, complete the Skills Focus questions below. Then use your answers and annotations from the questions to help you complete the Write activity.

◎ SKILLS FOCUS

1. In paragraph 1, identify words and phrases Patrick Henry uses to justify his speaking "freely, and without reserve." Explain how you would characterize the language and what it suggests about both Henry's audience and the situation facing the colonists.

2. In paragraph 3, Henry mentions the "war-like preparations" the British appear to be making. Describe Henry's ultimate purpose in discussing these preparations and how it helps advance his argument.

3. In paragraph 4, discuss how Henry's use of repetition, or repeated words or phrases, in his rhetoric helps advance his purpose and point of view.

4. At the close of his "Letter from Birmingham Jail," Martin Luther King, Jr. says, "Let us all hope that the dark clouds of racial prejudice will soon pass away and the deep fog of misunderstanding will be lifted from our fear drenched communities, and in some not too distant tomorrow the radiant stars of love and brotherhood will shine over our great nation with all their scintillating beauty." Compare and contrast the closing from this significant U.S. historic letter with Henry's message and rhetoric in paragraph 5 of his speech.

5. This speech by Patrick Henry is one of the most famous in U.S. history. Describe how Henry's language and style, as well as his awareness of his time and his audience, help to reinforce and enhance his message.

WRITE

RHETORICAL ANALYSIS: In the fifth stanza of Pat Mora's poem "A Voice," the speaker says,

You liked winning with words. You liked
writing speeches about patriotism and democracy.
You liked all the faces looking at you, all those eyes.
"How did I do it?" you ask me now. . . .

"Winning with words" is a goal in persuasive writing and speaking, and both Patrick Henry and Martin Luther King, Jr. use language to advocate for their ideas. Reflecting on Mora's poem and the shared concepts and themes in King's "Letter from Birmingham Jail" and Henry's "Speech to the Second Virginia Convention," discuss how a person's choice of words may be a matter of "life" and "death."

Extended Writing Project and Grammar

EXTENDED WRITING PROJECT
LITERARY ANALYSIS WRITING

Literary Analysis Writing Process: Plan

PLAN	DRAFT	REVISE	EDIT AND PUBLISH

The texts you have read in this unit grapple with the power of words. Language emerges in these texts as a powerful force, serving as a tool to unite past and future generations or operating as a means of achieving justice.

WRITING PROMPT

What is the power of language?

Select two or three works from this unit in which individuals' language has a powerful impact on themselves, another individual, or their community. In a literary analysis essay, make a claim about what exactly is the power of language and explain how that power is demonstrated in each of the selections. Cite evidence from the texts you have selected to support your position.

Writing to Sources

As you gather ideas and information from the texts in the unit, be sure to:

- include a claim;
- address counterclaims;
- use evidence from multiple sources; and
- avoid overly relying on one source.

Introduction to Literary Analysis Writing

A literary analysis consists of certain elements, including the following:

- a claim, or thesis
- valid reasons or points that support the claim
- textual evidence to support the reasons and the claim
- original commentary to explain the significance of the textual evidence

In a literary analysis, a writer analyzes how literary elements and devices work together to create meaning in one or more works of literature. Literary analysis is considered a form of argumentative writing in that the writer expresses a claim that states his or her position, or interpretation of the literary work, and then provides textual evidence and original commentary as justification for the claim.

Before you get started on your own literary analysis, read this essay that one student, Caroline, wrote in response to the writing prompt. As you read the Model, highlight and annotate the features of literary analysis writing that Caroline included in her essay.

NOTES

☰ STUDENT MODEL

The Power of Language

1   There is an old saying that "sticks and stones may break my bones, but words will never hurt me," but it isn't true. Words can be much more dangerous than sticks or stones. Words may not kill a person instantly, like a weapon—but, like a tool, they can shape the world. Words are powerful. They can change history by calling people to action. They can also change people's minds. The authors of "She Unnames Them," "Letter from Birmingham Jail," and "Speech to the Second Virginia Convention" all want to change the world, and they use words to bring about that change.

2   In "She Unnames Them" by Ursula K. Le Guin, Eve shows how powerful a name is even when it does not fit its owner. She explains that most of the animals never cared about the names Adam had given them. Yet some of the animals, especially pets and yaks, debate whether or not to keep their names. By unnaming the animals, Eve feels an unexpected "powerful" effect. She feels closer to but also more afraid of the animals. Then she realizes that she "could not now, in all conscience, make an exception for [herself]." She must give up her own name. Not wanting to seem ungrateful, she gives her name back to Adam. She tells him that it's "been really useful, but it doesn't exactly seem to fit very well lately." Adam does not seem to be listening. It is possible that Adam does not understand the power of words, probably because he is the one who gave Eve and the animals their names. Eve, however, now understands the power of language. As she leaves the garden, she realizes that her words must "be as slow, as new, as single, as tentative as the steps I took." Language is powerful, and the author confirms this idea by implying that Eve plans to use it carefully from now on.

3   While Le Guin seems to suggest using words with caution, revolutionary patriot Patrick Henry uses logical appeals and vivid language to persuade his audience in "Speech to the Second

Virginia Convention." When Henry delivered the speech in 1775, he was taking a big risk. The purpose of Henry's speech was to persuade his audience to declare independence from Britain. What Henry is suggesting is treasonous, but he feels so strongly about the "question of freedom or slavery" that he considers it treason to hold back his opinions. Henry shows respect for his audience by referring to them as "sir" and "gentlemen," but he argues that they are not seeing the world clearly. They are like people "who, having eyes, see not, and, having ears, hear not." He guides his listeners to see his point of view through logic. He asks rhetorical questions and then answers them. Yet it is his emotional language that is more persuasive. Throughout his speech, Henry uses the image of heavy chains to argue that the Americans are enslaved to Britain. He asks, "Is life so dear, or peace so sweet, as to be purchased at the price of chains and slavery?" He declares that "if we wish to be free," then "we must fight!" He ends his speech by speaking for himself: "I know not what course others may take; but as for me, give me liberty or give me death!" It is as if he does not care whether the others follow him; he knows that he will take courageous action.

4   Like Patrick Henry, Martin Luther King Jr. uses powerful language to address an injustice. King wrote "Letter from Birmingham Jail" after being arrested during a peaceful protest against racial segregation. King's letter is a response to white people who think that African Americans should not protest against inequality but should wait for it to be handled in the courts. Like Henry, King addresses his audience directly. For example, he asks questions: "You may well ask: 'Why direct action? Why sit ins, marches and so forth? Isn't negotiation a better path?'" He uses logic to explain how he ended up in jail. However, the most persuasive part of his argument comes from his use of powerful language to explain what injustice feels like to African Americans who experience "the stinging darts of segregation." He describes the pain of being told to be patient when "you have seen hate filled policemen curse, kick and even kill your black brothers and sisters." He expresses the pain of having to tell his daughter that she can't go to an amusement park because she is black and of having to live a life "plagued with inner fears and outer resentments." Yet he ends his letter by imagining a day in which "the South will recognize its real heroes"—those people who peacefully and courageously fought for their civil rights. He describes them as

Please note that excerpts and passages in the StudySync® library and this workbook are intended as touchstones to generate interest in an author's work. The excerpts and passages do not substitute for the reading of entire texts, and StudySync® strongly recommends that students seek out and purchase the whole literary or informational work in order to experience it as the author intended. Links to online resellers are available in our digital library. In addition, complete works may be ordered through an authorized reseller by filling out and returning to StudySync® the order form enclosed in this workbook.

Reading & Writing Companion   105

"bringing our nation back to those great wells of democracy which were dug deep by the founding fathers." As a result of King's powerful language, others could share his vision of the world as it is and as it might be.

5   Words are everywhere. It's easy to tune them out or think that they don't mean much. But when life turns serious, and there are injustices and wrongs to fix, people rely on the power of words. In "Speech to the Second Virginia Convention" and "Letter from Birmingham Jail," Patrick Henry and Martin Luther King Jr. describe terrible injustices and challenge their audiences to think about the world in a new way and to take action. In "She Unnames Them," Eve recognizes the power of naming and finds freedom by giving up a name she didn't choose. She decides that she's up to the challenge of using language thoughtfully and carefully instead of chattering. All have learned, as have we in reading these three selections, that language can be an important and powerful tool for changing the world in serious ways.

✎ WRITE

Writers often take notes about their ideas before they sit down to write an essay. Think about what you've learned so far about literary analysis to help you begin prewriting.

- **Purpose:** Think about the texts you have read in this unit. What two or three works would you like to explore further in a literary analysis?

- **Audience:** Who will read your literary analysis? What type of language and style should you use for this audience?

- **Textual Evidence:** Is there any particular passage that immediately comes to mind that exemplifies the power of language?

- **Analysis:** What do you think that passage suggests about the power of language?

- **Claim:** How can you use the passage you have identified and your commentary on it to begin to formulate the claim of your literary analysis?

Response Instructions

Use the questions in the bulleted list to write a one-paragraph summary. Your summary should help guide you in the planning and writing of your literary analysis essay.

Don't worry about including all of the details now; focus only on the most essential and important elements. You will refer to this short summary as you continue through the steps of the writing process.

Skill: Organizing
Argumentative Writing

••• CHECKLIST FOR ORGANIZING ARGUMENTATIVE WRITING

As you consider how to organize your writing for your argumentative essay, use the following questions as a guide:

- Have I identified my claim or claims and the evidence that supports it?

- Have I identified reasons for my claim?

- Have I identified any counterclaims that I will need to address?

- Have I identified the textual evidence that will support my reasons?

Follow these steps to organize your argumentative essay in a way that establishes clear relationships among claim(s), counterclaims, reasons, and evidence:

- Identify your precise, or specific, claim or claims and the reasons to support each one.

- Identify textual evidence that will support each reason.

- Identify any counterclaims, as needed.

- Choose an organizational structure that establishes clear relationships among claims, reasons, and the evidence presented to support your claim.

YOUR TURN

Read the quotations from a student's literary analysis essay on "In Between Cultures: A Granddaughter's Advantage" below. Then, complete the chart by matching each quotation with its correct place in the outline.

	Quotation Options
A	Likewise, the speaker in Mohja Kahf's "My Grandmother Washes Her Feet in the Sink of the Bathroom at Sears" must choose from a host of available **options**, not the least of which is "a clash of civilizations" or "the great common ground."
B	Through her portrayal of the granddaughter, Kahf challenges the commonly held belief that hyphenated Americans are torn between two cultures.
C	The speaker must reconcile seemingly irreconcilable perspectives: on the one hand, that of the customers. . . .
D	In this way, the granddaughter's in-between identity provides her with a unique perspective—she sees both sides—and this proves to be advantageous.
E	If anyone deserves credit for this coming together, however, it is not Sears, Roebuck, and Company, it is the granddaughter.
F	The granddaughter has opened the door "for everyone" by using her unique ability to communicate across language and culture.

Outline	Quotation
Introductory Statement:	
Thesis:	
Main Idea/Reason 1:	
Main Idea/Reason 2:	
Main Idea/Reason 3:	
Conclusion:	

Please note that excerpts and passages in the StudySync® library and this workbook are intended as touchstones to generate interest in an author's work. The excerpts and passages do not substitute for the reading of entire texts, and StudySync® strongly recommends that students seek out and purchase the whole literary or informational work in order to experience it as the author intended. Links to online resellers are available in our digital library. In addition, complete works may be ordered through an authorized reseller by filling out and returning to StudySync® the order form enclosed in this workbook.

Reading & Writing Companion 109

YOUR TURN

Complete the chart below by writing a short summary of what will happen in each section of your literary analysis.

My Literary Analysis	
Purpose, Audience, Topic, Context:	
Introductory Statement:	
Thesis:	
Main Idea/Reason 1:	
Main Idea/Reason 2:	
Main Idea/Reason 3:	

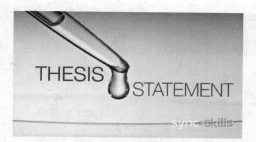

Skill:
Thesis Statement

••• CHECKLIST FOR THESIS STATEMENT

Before you begin writing your thesis statement for your argumentative essay, ask yourself the following questions:

- What is the prompt asking me to write about?

- What claim do I want to make about the topic of this essay?

- Is my claim precise? How is it specific to my topic?

- Does my thesis statement introduce the body of my essay?

- Where should I place my thesis statement?

Here are some methods to introduce and develop a topic as well as a precise claim:

- think about your central claim of your essay

  > identify a clear claim you want to introduce, thinking about:

    o how closely your claim is related to your topic and specific to your supporting details

    o any alternate or opposing claims (counterclaims)

  > identify as many claims and counterclaims as you intend to prove

- your thesis statement should:

  > let the reader anticipate the content of your essay

  > begin your essay in an organized manner

  > present your opinion clearly

  > respond completely to the writing prompt

- consider the best placement for your thesis statement

  > if your response is short, you may want to get right to the point and present your thesis statement in the first sentence of the essay

  > if your response is longer (as in a formal essay), you can build up your thesis statement and place it at the end of your introductory paragraph

Copyright © BookheadEd Learning, LLC

Reading & Writing
Companion

⟳ YOUR TURN

Read the sentences below. Then, complete the chart by sorting them into those that are thesis statements and those that are supporting details.

	Sentence Options
A	When making an argument, an author's rhetoric can have as much of an impact on the audience as the content of the ideas.
B	Names demonstrate the power of language.
C	Dr. Martin Luther King Jr.'s "Letter from Birmingham Jail" is effective because it uses powerful imagery such as "the stinging darts of segregation."
D	Language is always a powerful tool, but it is most powerful when effective imagery is used to paint a picture in readers' or listeners' minds.
E	In "She Unnames Them," Eve realizes she must give up her own name because it no longer fits her.
F	Patrick Henry asks and answers rhetorical questions in order to persuade people that independence from Britain is a good idea.

Thesis Statements	Supporting Details

✏ WRITE

Use the steps in the checklist to draft a thesis statement for your literary analysis.

Skill: Reasons and Relevant Evidence

••• CHECKLIST FOR REASONS AND RELEVANT EVIDENCE

As you begin to determine what reasons and relevant evidence will support your claim(s), use the following questions as a guide:

- Is my claim precise, specific, and clearly stated?

- How is my claim different from any alternate or opposing claims? How can I make my claim more specific to my topic and ideas?

- What are the relationships between the claims, counterclaims, reasons, and evidence I have presented? What kinds of transitional devices or organizational patterns might improve these relationships?

- What is my counterclaim? How can I use it to strengthen my claim?

Use the following steps as a guide to help you introduce a precise claim(s), distinguish the claim(s) from alternate or opposing claims, and create an organization that establishes clear relationships among argument elements:

- identify the precise claim or claims you will make in your argument, refine it by:

  > eliminating any gaps of information or vague ideas

  > using vocabulary that clarifies your ideas

  > evaluating how it is distinguished, or different, from other claims and counterclaims on your topic

- assess any connections between your claim and the counterclaim, which is another claim made to refute or disprove a previous claim

- choose or create an organizational pattern, such as compare and contrast, that will establish clear relationships among claim(s), counterclaims, reasons, and evidence

YOUR TURN

Read each piece of textual evidence from "She Unnames Them" below. Then, complete the chart by sorting them into those that are relevant and those that are not relevant to the writing topic of "the power of language."

Textual Evidence	
A	They seemed far closer than when their names had stood between myself and them like a clear barrier: so close that my fear of them and their fear of me became one same fear.
B	I put some things away and fiddled around a little, but he continued to do what he was doing and to take no notice of anything else.
C	But as soon as they understood that the issue was precisely one of individual choice, and that anybody who wanted to be called Rover, or Froufrou, or Polly, or even Birdie in the personal sense, was perfectly free to do so . . .
D	He was fitting parts together, and said, without looking around, "O.K., fine dear. When's dinner?"

Relevant Evidence	Not Relevant Evidence

 YOUR TURN

Complete the chart below by identifying 1) three texts you may want to write about; 2) reasons for choosing each text; and 3) relevant evidence from each text to help develop your own writing ideas.

Text	Reasons	Relevant Evidence

Literary Analysis Writing Process: Draft

| PLAN | DRAFT | REVISE | EDIT AND PUBLISH |

You have already made progress toward writing your literary analysis. Now it is time to draft your literary analysis.

✏ WRITE

Use your plan and other responses in your Binder to draft your literary analysis. After rereading the prompt, you may also think of new ideas as you begin drafting. Feel free to explore those new ideas as you have them. You can also ask yourself these questions to ensure that your writing is focused, organized, and developed:

Draft Checklist:

☐ **Focused**: Have I introduced my claim clearly in a thesis statement? Have I included only relevant evidence to support my claim, and nothing extraneous that might confuse my readers?

☐ **Organized**: Have I organized my analysis in a way that makes sense with the texts I have chosen? Have I established clear relationships among claims, counterclaims, reasons, and evidence?

☐ **Developed**: Have I clearly stated reasons that support my claim? Have I identified counterclaims and alternate claims in a way my audience can follow? Is my evidence sufficient?

Before you submit your draft, read it over carefully. You want to be sure that you've responded to all aspects of the prompt.

Please note that excerpts and passages in the StudySync® library and this workbook are intended as touchstones to generate interest in an author's work. The excerpts and passages do not substitute for the reading of entire texts, and StudySync® strongly recommends that students seek out and purchase the whole literary or informational work in order to experience it as the author intended. Links to online resellers are available in our digital library. In addition, complete works may be ordered through an authorized reseller by filling out and returning to StudySync® the order form enclosed in this workbook.

Reading & Writing Companion 115

Here is Caroline's draft of her literary analysis. As you read, notice how Caroline develops her draft to be focused, organized, and developed. As Caroline continues to revise and edit her literary analysis, she will introduce counterclaims, find and improve weak spots in her writing, as well as correct any language or punctuation mistakes.

NOTES

STUDENT MODEL: FIRST DRAFT

The Power of Language

~~Words are powerful things. They can change the world. They can change people's minds. Words can hurt just as much as stick or stones, as the old saying goes. The authors of "She Unnames Them," "Letter from Birmingham Jail," and "Speech to the Second Virginia Convention" all want to change the world, so they use their words.~~

There is an old saying that "sticks and stones may break my bones, but words will never hurt me," but it isn't true. Words can be much more dangerous than sticks or stones. Words may not kill a person instantly, like a weapon—but, like a tool, they can shape the world. Words are powerful. They can change history by calling people to action. They can also change people's minds. The authors of "She Unnames Them," "Letter from Birmingham Jail," and "Speech to the Second Virginia Convention" all want to change the world, and they use words to bring about that change.

In "She Unnames Them" by Ursula K. Le Guin, Eve learns that most of the animals never cared about the names Adam had given them. By unaming the animals, Eve feels an unexpected "powerful" effect. She feels closer to but also more afraid of the animals. She realizes that she must renounce her own name. She tries to give her name back to Adam. He doesn't seem to be listening; because he pays no attention to her words. As she leaves the garden, she realizes that her words must "be as slow, as new, as single, as tentative as the steps I took."

Patrick Henry uses strong language to get his listeners to change their minds in "Speech to the Second Virginia Convention." When he delivered the speech in 1775, he was taking a big risk. The purpose of his speech was to persuade his audience to declare independence from Britain. What Henry is suggesting is treasonous, but he feels so

Skill: Introductions

Caroline understands that she needs to add a more interesting "hook." She decides to start with an old saying, rather than placing this saying several sentences into the paragraph. Next, she decides to add sentences to help explain how and why words are powerful and even dangerous. Last, she crafts a stronger, clearer claim and a more complete introductory paragraph.

strongly about "the question of freedom or slavery" that he considers it is treason to hold back his opinions. Henry shows respect for his audience, but he argues that they are not seeing the world clearly. He guides his listeners to see his point of view through logic. He asks rhetorical questions and then answers them. Yet it is his emotional language that is more persuasive. Throughout his speech, he uses the image of heavy chains to argue that the Americans are enslaved to Britian. He asks, "is life so dear, or peace so sweet, as to be purchased at the price of chains and slavery?" He declares that "if we wish to be free" then "we must fight!" he ends his speech by speaking for himself: "I know not what course others may take; but as for me, give me liberty or give me death! It was like he didn't care whether the others folow him, he knows what he will do. He has convinced himself to take couragous action.

~~King wrote "Letter from Birmingham Jail" after being arrested during a peacefull protest against racial segregation. His letter is a response to white people. They think that African Americans should not protest against inequality. Instead they should wait for it to be handled in the courts. King addresses his audience directly and asks questions. He uses logic to explain how he ended up in jail. The most persuasive part of his argument comes from his use of powerful language to explain what injustice feels like to African Americans. He expresses the pain of having to tell his daughter that she can't go to an amusement park because she is black. he paints a picture of a world that is unjust and dangerous for people of color. He ends his letter by imagining a day in which "the South will recognize its real heroes." He is talking about those people who peacefully—And courageously— fought for their civil Rights.~~

Like Patrick Henry, Martin Luther King Jr. uses powerful language to address an injustice. King wrote "Letter from Birmingham Jail" after being arrested during a peaceful protest against racial segregation. King's letter is a response to white people who think that African Americans should not protest against inequality but should wait for it to be handled in the courts. Like Henry, King addresses his audience directly. For example, he asks questions: "You may well ask, 'Why direct action? Why sit ins, marches and so forth? Isn't negotiation a better path?'" He uses logic to explain how he ended up in jail. However, the most persuasive part of his argument comes

Skill:
Transitions

Caroline's new topic sentence—"Like Patrick Henry, Martin Luther King Jr. uses powerful language to address an injustice"—introduces the main idea developed in this paragraph. The transition "Like Patrick Henry" makes a connection to another author whose text Caroline discusses in an earlier paragraph.

from his use of powerful language to explain what injustice feels like to African Americans who experience "the stinging darts of segregation." He describes the pain of being told to be patient when "you have seen hate filled policemen curse, kick and even kill your black brothers and sisters." He expresses the pain of having to tell his daughter that she can't go to an amusement park because she is black and of having to live a life "plagued with inner fears and outer resentments." Yet he ends his letter by imagining a day in which "the South will recognize its real heroes"—those people who peacefully and courageously fought for their civil rights. He describes them as "bringing our nation back to those great wells of democracy which were dug deep by the founding fathers." As a result of King's powerful language, others could share his vision of the world as it is and as it might be.

Skill:
Conclusions

Caroline notices that her conclusion simply restates her original claim almost exactly as it appears in the introduction. She rephrases the claim in the conclusion to show the depth of her knowledge about the topic. She adds some of her own thoughts in order to make an impression on the audience at the end.

~~All three authors want to change the world, so they use their words. The selections "She Unnames Them," "Speech to the Second Virginia Convention," and "Letter from Birmingham Jail," all use powerful words to say important stuff about the world. Patrick Henry and Martin Luther King Jr. talk about injustices and challenge their audiences to think about the world in a new way. The character of Eve recognizes the power of naming and finds freedom by giving up her name.~~

Words are everywhere. It's easy to tune them out or think that they don't mean much. But when life turns serious, and there are injustices and wrongs to fix, people rely on the power of words. In "Speech to the Second Virginia Convention" and "Letter from Birmingham Jail," Patrick Henry and Martin Luther King Jr. describe terrible injustices and challenge their audiences to think about the world in a new way and to take action. In "She Unnames Them," Eve recognizes the power of naming and finds freedom by giving up a name she didn't choose. She decides that she's up to the challenge of using language thoughtfully and carefully instead of chattering. All have learned, as have we in reading these three selections, that language can be an important and powerful tool for changing the world in serious ways.

Skill:
Introductions

••• CHECKLIST FOR INTRODUCTIONS

Before you write your introduction, ask yourself the following questions:

- What is my claim? Have I recognized opposing claims that disagree with mine or have a different perspective? How can I use them to make my own claim more precise?

- How can I introduce my topic? How have I organized complex ideas, concepts, and information to make important connections and distinctions?

- How will I "hook" my reader's interest? I might:

  > start with an attention-grabbing statement

  > begin with an intriguing question

Below are two strategies to help you introduce your precise claim and topic clearly in an introduction:

- Peer Discussion

  > Talk about your topic with a partner, explaining what you already know and your ideas about your topic.

  > Write down notes and talk about how to state your claim or thesis.

  > Briefly state your precise claim or thesis, establishing how it is different from alternative claims and counterclaims about your topic.

  > Ask about ideas to "hook" a reader.

- Freewriting

  > Freewrite for 10 minutes about your topic. Don't worry about grammar, punctuation, or having fully formed ideas. The point of freewriting is to discover ideas.

  > Review your notes and draft your claim or thesis.

  > Establish how your thesis is different from alternate claims about your topic.

  > Brainstorm ways to "hook" your reader.

Please note that excerpts and passages in the StudySync® library and this workbook are intended as touchstones to generate interest in an author's work. The excerpts and passages do not substitute for the reading of entire texts, and StudySync® strongly recommends that students seek out and purchase the whole literary or informational work in order to experience it as the author intended. Links to online resellers are available in our digital library. In addition, complete works may be ordered through an authorized reseller by filling out and returning to StudySync® the order form enclosed in this workbook.

Reading & Writing Companion

119

⟳ YOUR TURN

Choose the best answer to each question.

1. Which of the following belongs in an introductory paragraph?

   ○ A. a concluding statement to sum up the argument
   ○ B. a list of reasons to support a claim
   ○ C. relevant supporting evidence to justify a claim
   ○ D. a thesis statement containing a claim

2. Below is Caroline's introduction from a previous draft. The meaning of the underlined sentence is unclear. How can she rewrite the underlined sentence to make her idea clearer?

   <u>Words are only made of air and sound but are so important.</u> They can change the world and people's minds. Words can hurt just as much as stick or stones, like that old saying goes. The authors of "She Unnames Them," "Letter from Birmingham Jail," and "Speech to the Second Virginia Convention" all try to change the world by using their words.

   ○ A. Words are powerful tools.
   ○ B. Words are made of nothing, but they have a big impact.
   ○ C. Words can be whispered or shouted.
   ○ D. Words are things that most people can't live without.

✏ WRITE

Use the questions in the checklist to revise the introduction of your literary analysis to meet the needs of the purpose, audience, topic, and context.

Skill:
Transitions

••• CHECKLIST FOR TRANSITIONS

Before you revise your current draft to include transitions, think about:

- the key ideas you discuss in your body paragraphs
- the relationships among your claim(s), reasons, and evidence
- the relationship between your claim(s) and counterclaims
- the logical progression of your argument

Next, reread your current draft and note areas in your essay where:

- the relationships between your claim(s), counterclaims, and the reasons and evidence are unclear, identifying places where you could add linking words or other transitional devices to make your argument more cohesive. Look for:

  > sudden jumps in your ideas

  > breaks between paragraphs where the ideas in the next paragraph are not logically following from the previous

Revise your draft to use words, phrases, and clauses to link the major sections of the text, create cohesion, and clarify the relationships between claim(s) and reasons, between reasons and evidence, and between claim(s) and counterclaims, using the following the questions as a guide:

- Are there unifying relationships between the claims, reasons, and the evidence I present in my argument?
- How do my claim(s) and counterclaims relate?
- Have I clarified, or made clear, these relationships?
- What linking words (such as conjunctions), phrases, or clauses could I add to my argument to clarify the relationships between the claims, reasons, and evidence I present?

YOUR TURN

Choose the best answer to each question.

1. Below is a body paragraph from a previous draft of Caroline's literary analysis. Caroline has not included an effective topic sentence. Which of the following could replace the underlined sentence in this body paragraph and provide the most effective transition to the ideas that follow?

> <u>In "She Unnames Them," the main character is the first woman Eve.</u> Eve understands that the names that Adam has given her and all of the world's creatures don't fit them. Without telling Adam, she unnames all the animals and herself. She is surprised by the powerful feeling she gets when names are removed. She tries to give back her name, but Adam doesn't listen. Eve wishes she could explain her decision to him. In the end, Eve realizes that her own words do matter. They are too precious to waste on someone who doesn't listen.

- ○ A. In "She Unnames Them," the main character is the first woman Eve, who frees the animals from their names and gives up her own name as an act of rebellion.
- ○ B. Authors tend to think that words are important because words are the way they communicate their ideas to others.
- ○ C. In "She Unnames Them," the characters are unable to use words to communicate well with each other, and as a result, the story is difficult to read.
- ○ D. In "She Unnames Them," the author uses the character of Eve to demonstrate how words can have great power and should be used sparingly.

2. Below is a body paragraph from a previous draft of Caroline's literary analysis. Caroline would like to add a transition word or phrase to help readers move from sentence 4 to sentence 5. Which of these is the most effective transition to add to the beginning of sentence 5?

> (1) Like Martin Luther King Jr., Patrick Henry uses powerful language to address injustice in "Speech to the Second Virginia Convention." (2) Henry's purpose was to persuade members of the convention to rebel against the king of England. (3) He feels so strongly about "the question of freedom or slavery" that he considers it treason to hold back his opinions. (4) He uses both logical and emotional appeals. (5) His emotional appeal is more effective. (6) When Henry declares "give me liberty or give me death," he shows his true, heartfelt feelings. (7) Even readers today feel moved by the passion behind his words.

○ A. Finally,

○ B. However,

○ C. Therefore,

○ D. As a result,

✏️ **WRITE**

Use the questions in the checklist to revise one of your body paragraphs in order to clarify its claim or counterclaim and add cohesion and establish relationships between ideas through the use of transitions.

Skill:
Conclusions

••• CHECKLIST FOR CONCLUSIONS

Before you write your conclusion, ask yourself the following questions:

- How can I restate the thesis or main idea?
- How can I write my conclusion so that it supports and follows from the information I presented?
- How can I communicate the importance of my topic? What information do I need?

Below are two strategies to help you provide a concluding statement or section that follows from and supports the information or explanation presented:

- Peer Discussion

    > After you have written your introduction and body paragraphs, talk with a partner about what you want readers to remember; take notes.

    > Think about how you can articulate, or express, the significance of your topic in the conclusion.

        o Restate any ideas from people who are experts on your topic.

        o Note possible implications if something is done or is not accomplished.

    > Rephrase your claim to show the depth of your knowledge and support for the information you presented.

    > Write your conclusion.

- Freewriting

    > Freewrite for 10 minutes to discover ideas about what to include in your conclusion. Don't worry about grammar, punctuation, or having fully formed ideas.

    > Follow the last three steps as you would for Peer Discussion, above.

YOUR TURN

Choose the best answer to each question.

1. Which of the following belongs in a concluding paragraph?

   ○ A. a statement to sum up the argument and demonstrate that a claim is valid, or true
   ○ B. reasons and relevant evidence to support a claim
   ○ C. transitions to link major sections of text
   ○ D. a "hook" and the first appearance of the thesis statement containing a claim

2. Below is Caroline's conclusion from a previous draft. Her closing sentence is weak. Which of these sentences could replace her final sentence, which is underlined, to provide a more effective closing to her literary analysis?

> All three authors show the power of language. The authors of "She Unnames Them," "Speech to the Second Virginia Convention," and "Letter from Birmingham Jail" use words to say something important about the world. Patrick Henry and Martin Luther King Jr. talk about injustices and challenge their audiences to think. Eve understands that because language is powerful, she will use it carefully from now on. <u>Because our words are important and precious, we should think carefully before speaking.</u>

   ○ A. Don't you think it's important to use powerful words when it's time to change the world?
   ○ B. These three selections help show that words can be powerful tools for changing the world.
   ○ C. Let's watch how we use our words at all times because they are so important.
   ○ D. Like Eve, maybe we should all choose our words more carefully in the future.

 WRITE

Use the questions in the checklist to revise the conclusion of your literary analysis to meet the needs of the purpose, audience, topic, and context.

Please note that excerpts and passages in the StudySync® library and this workbook are intended as touchstones to generate interest in an author's work. The excerpts and passages do not substitute for the reading of entire texts, and StudySync® strongly recommends that students seek out and purchase the whole literary or informational work in order to experience it as the author intended. Links to online resellers are available in our digital library. In addition, complete works may be ordered through an authorized reseller by filling out and returning to StudySync® the order form enclosed in this workbook.

Reading & Writing Companion 125

Literary Analysis Writing Process: Revise

PLAN	DRAFT	REVISE	EDIT AND PUBLISH

You have written a draft of your literary analysis. You have also received input from your peers about how to improve it. Now you are going to revise your draft.

◀◀ REVISION GUIDE

Examine your draft to find areas for revision. Keep in mind your purpose and audience as you revise for clarity, development, organization, and style. Use the guide below to help you review:

Review	Revise	Example
Clarity		
Label each pronoun to make it clear to whom you are referring.	Use the authors' or characters' names to identify who you are talking about.	When ~~he~~ Henry delivered the speech in 1775, he was taking a big risk. The purpose of ~~his~~ Henry's speech was to persuade his audience to declare independence from Britain.
Development		
Identify the textual evidence that supports your claims and include commentary. Annotate places where you feel that there is not enough textual evidence to support your ideas or where you have failed to provide commentary.	Focus on a single idea or claim and add your personal reflections in the form of commentary or support in the form of textual evidence.	Henry shows respect for his audience by referring to them as "sir" and "gentlemen," but he argues that they are not seeing the world clearly. They are like people "who, having eyes, see not, and, having ears, hear not."

Review	Revise	Example
Organization		
Review your body paragraphs. Identify and annotate any sentences that don't flow in a clear or logical way.	Reorganize or rewrite sentences so that each paragraph progresses in a logical sequence, starting with a clear topic sentence and including transitions as needed. Delete details that are repetitive or not essential to the claim.	By unnaming the animals, Eve feels an unexpected "powerful" effect. She feels closer to but also more afraid of the animals. ~~She~~ Then she realizes that she must renounce her own name. When she ~~She~~ tries to give her name back to Adam, ~~. He~~ he does not seem to be listening~~;~~ ~~because he pays no attention to her words~~.
Style: Word Choice		
Look for everyday words and phrases that could be replaced with academic language, such as literary terms, or more precise language.	Replace everyday language with academic terms, such as *logical appeal*, *persuade*, and *audience*.	Patrick Henry uses ~~strong~~ logical appeals and vivid language to ~~get his listeners to change their minds~~ persuade his audience in "Speech to the Second Virginia Convention."
Style: Sentence Effectiveness		
Read your literary analysis aloud. Annotate places where you have too many long or short sentences in a row.	Shorten longer sentences for clarity or emphasis. Revise short sentences by linking them together.	His letter is a response to white people~~.~~ ~~They~~ who think that African Americans should not protest against inequality~~.~~ ~~Instead they~~ but should wait for it to be handled in the courts.

✏ WRITE

Use the guide above, as well as your peer reviews, to help you evaluate your literary analysis to determine areas that should be revised.

Skill:
Style

••• CHECKLIST FOR STYLE

First, reread the draft of your literary analysis essay and identify the following:

- slang, colloquialisms, contractions, abbreviations, or a conversational tone
- areas where you could use domain-specific or academic language in order to help persuade or inform your readers
- the use of first person (*I*) or second person (*you*)
- areas where you could vary sentence structure and length, emphasizing compound, complex, and compound-complex sentences
- statements that express judgment or emotion, rather than an objective tone that relies on facts and evidence
- incorrect uses of the conventions of standard English for grammar, spelling, capitalization, and punctuation

Establish and maintain a formal style in your essay, using the following questions as a guide:

> Have I avoided slang in favor of academic language?

> Did I consistently used a third-person perspective, using third-person pronouns (*he*, *she*, *they*)?

> Have I maintained an objective tone without expressing my own judgments and emotions?

> Have I used varied sentence lengths and different sentence structures?

   o Where should I make some sentences longer by using conjunctions to connect independent clauses, dependent clauses, and phrases?

   o Where should I make some sentences shorter by separating independent clauses?

> Did I follow the conventions of standard English?

⟳ YOUR TURN

Choose the best answer to each question.

1. Below is a section from a previous draft of Caroline's literary analysis. She wants to add some style to the paragraph. Which sentence could she add after sentence 4 to achieve that goal?

> (1) Patrick Henry's "Speech to the Second Virginia Convention" is a stirring call to war. (2) He begins by addressing his audience directly and politely. (3) He asks and answers rhetorical questions to help his listeners see the logic of his thinking. (4) However, he also uses emotional appeals effectively. (5) He declares that "there is no retreat but submission and slavery!" (6) He exclaims that no matter what the others at the convention will do, his choice is "give me liberty or give me death!"

- ○ A. I think Henry's speech is basically a call for his colleagues at the convention to commit treason.
- ○ B. Henry's mixture of logical and emotional appeals makes his argument interesting to read.
- ○ C. Henry's use of the metaphor of the chains effectively illustrates his passionate stance.
- ○ D. Henry allows his own personal feelings to erupt throughout the speech.

2. Caroline wants to improve the topic sentence of a paragraph from a previous draft of her literary analysis. She wants the topic sentence to use formal style to more clearly express her analysis. Which sentence is a better replacement for the underlined sentence?

> I get the feeling that Eve's relationship with language is the focus of the story "She Unnames Them." Eve discovers that most of the animals do not care about their names. The names are unnecessary. She feels an unexpected "powerful" effect from taking away their names. Then she realizes that she must give up her own name. She is not sure how she feels about it. It doesn't "fit," but she doesn't want to seem "ungrateful."

- ○ A. Eve's decision to unname the animals and leave the garden is a rewriting of an ancient biblical tale.
- ○ B. I think Eve's determination to unname the animals and herself falters when she must speak to Adam in person.
- ○ C. Eve's main discovery in the story is that language, especially names, can be powerful, and she is right.
- ○ D. Eve's uncertainty about her relationship to language indicates an inner conflict that is key to understanding the story.

WRITE

Use the steps in the checklist to add to or revise the language of your thesis, use of textual evidence, and a paragraph or section of your analysis to demonstrate a formal style and objective tone.

Grammar: Basic Spelling Rules I

Examples

Rule	Text	Explanation
When adding a suffix that begins with a vowel to a word that ends with a silent **e**, usually drop the **e**. When adding a suffix that begins with a consonant to a word that ends with a silent **e**, keep the **e**.	Therefore **begrudging** neither augury Nor other **divination** that is thine, O save thyself, thy country, and thy king, Save all from this **defilement** of blood shed. *Oedipus Rex*	*Begrudging* drops the final silent *e* of *begrudge*, because the suffix starts with a vowel. *Divination* drops the final silent *e* of *divine*, because the suffix starts with a vowel. *Defilement* keeps the silent *e*, because the suffix starts with a consonant.
Always keep the original spelling of the word when you add a prefix.	It is the Nation's resilience, not its rigidity, that Texas sees reflected in the flag—and it is that resilience that we **reassert** today. Texas v. Johnson	The prefix *re-* does not change the spelling of the base word *assert*.
When **i** and **e** appear after a **c**, the **e** usually comes before the **i**. However, there are exceptions to this rule.	Let us not, I beseech you, sir, **deceive** ourselves. Speech to the Second Virginia Convention	When following a *c*, *e* comes before *i*.
When a word ends in a consonant + **y**, change the **y** to **i** before adding a suffix.	America is rapidly losing its position as leader of the world simply because the Democratic Administration has **pitifully** failed to provide effective leadership. Remarks to the Senate in Support of a Declaration of Conscience	The *y* at the end of *pity* is changed to an *i* before adding the suffix *-fully*.

YOUR TURN

1. How should the spelling error in this sentence be corrected?

> The democratic rules of debate and voting are violated when Napoleon has the conciet to use his trained dogs to viciously attack Snowball, seize control, and monopolize power.

- ○ A. Change **conciet** to **conceit**.
- ○ B. Change **violated** to **violateed**.
- ○ C. Change **monopolize** to **monopalize**.
- ○ D. No change needs to be made to this sentence.

2. How should the spelling error in this sentence be corrected?

> The bedraggled chihuahua in the torrential rain was the most pityable creature imaginable.

- ○ A. Change **torrential** to **torrencial**.
- ○ B. Change **pityable** to **pitiable**.
- ○ C. Change **imaginable** to **imagineable**.
- ○ D. No change needs to be made to this sentence.

3. How should the spelling error in this sentence be corrected?

> By constantly discusing their shared dream, Ryne and Lennie inspire themselves to work toward an incredibly difficult goal.

- ○ A. Change **constantly** to **constanly**.
- ○ B. Change **discusing** to **discussing**.
- ○ C. Change **incredibly** to **incredibally**.
- ○ D. No change needs to be made to this sentence.

4. How should the spelling error in this sentence be corrected?

> Technological advances have brought miraculous solutions to problems as well as consequences that could not be forseen.

- ○ A. Change **Technological** to **Technologycal**.
- ○ B. Change **solutions** to **soluteions**.
- ○ C. Change **forseen** to **foreseen**.
- ○ D. No change needs to be made to this sentence.

Grammar: Independent and Dependent Clauses

A clause is a group of words that has both a subject (noun) and a predicate (verb). A clause can function as a sentence by itself or as part of a sentence.

Independent or Main Clause

An independent clause is also called a main clause. An independent or main clause has a subject and a predicate and expresses a complete thought. It can stand alone as a sentence.

Incorrect	Correct
visited the beach	The family visited the beach.
the sleepy teen	The sleepy teen turned off his alarm clock.

Dependent or Subordinate Clause

A dependent clause is also called a subordinate clause. A dependent or subordinate clause has a subject and a predicate, but it does not express a complete thought. It cannot stand alone as a sentence.

Dependent, or subordinate, clauses usually begin with a subordinating conjunction, such as *when*, *since*, *because*, *after*, or *while*. They may also begin with a relative pronoun, such as *who*, *whose*, *whom*, *which*, *that*, or *what*, or with a relative adverb, such as *when*, *where*, or *why*. In some subordinate clauses, the connecting word also serves as the subject of the clause.

Text	Explanation
Never shall I forget that night, the first night in camp, **that turned my life into one long night seven times sealed.** *Night*	**That** is a relative pronoun. It stands in for the noun *night*. It begins the subordinate clause. **Turned** is the verb in the subordinate clause. It tells what the night did.
Do I have the right to represent the multitudes **who have perished**? Nobel Prize Acceptance Speech	**Who** is a relative pronoun. It stands in for the noun *multitudes*. It begins the subordinate clause. **Perished** is the verb in the subordinate clause. Along with the auxiliary verb **have**, it tells what happened to the multitudes.

YOUR TURN

1. How should this sentence be changed?

   Because Jim and Clare went to a Chicago Cubs' game that was played in Wrigley Field.

   ○ A. Insert a period after **game**.
   ○ B. Delete the word **because**.
   ○ C. Replace **that** with **which**.
   ○ D. No change needs to be made to this sentence.

2. How should this sentence be changed?

   The movie that Sue rented was very creepy.

   ○ A. Delete **was very creepy**.
   ○ B. Insert **since** before **the**.
   ○ C. Delete **that Sue rented**.
   ○ D. No change needs to be made to this sentence.

3. How should this sentence be changed?

   Chili is Lila's favorite food it's cold outside.

   ○ A. Insert **whenever** before **chili**.
   ○ B. Insert **when** after **food**.
   ○ C. Insert **that** after **chili**.
   ○ D. No change needs to be made to this sentence.

4. How should this sentence be changed?

   Becka's orange shirt, which Tom had given her for her birthday.

   ○ A. Delete **Becka's orange shirt**.
   ○ B. Insert a **comma** and **ripped** after **birthday**.
   ○ C. Replace **which** with **because**.
   ○ D. No change needs to be made to this sentence.

COLONS AND
SEMICOLONS
SEMICOLONS
sync•skills

Grammar: Semicolons

A semicolon [;] connects groups of words in a sentence. Most often, a semicolon is used to join independent clauses that are not already connected with a comma and a coordinating conjunction, such as *and*, *but*, *so*, or *or*. When a semicolon is used in this way, do not use a coordinating conjunction as well. Also, keep in mind that both sentence parts need to be independent clauses.

Correct	Incorrect
Sonia was deeply committed to doing her work well; she consistently applied all her abilities to the task at hand.	Sonia was deeply committed to doing her work well; and she consistently applied all her abilities to the task at hand.
Tom Hanks is a talented and appealing actor, especially in the movie *Forrest Gump*.	Tom Hanks is a talented and appealing actor; especially in the movie *Forrest Gump*.

Follow these additional rules when using semicolons:

Rule	Text
When a semicolon is used between independent clauses, the clauses must be closely related in thought.	The few birds seen anywhere were moribund; they trembled violently and could not fly. *Silent Spring*
Use a semicolon to join two independent clauses with a conjunctive adverb (such as *however*) or another transition word or phrase (such as *for example*). A comma may follow the transition word or phrase.	The animals listened first to Napoleon, then to Snowball, and could not make up their minds which was right; indeed, they always found themselves in agreement with the one who was speaking at the moment. *Animal Farm*
Use a semicolon to separate items in a series when one or more of the items already contains commas.	She survives him, as do his brothers Malachy and Alphie, both of Manhattan, and his brother Mike, of San Francisco; his daughter, Maggie McCourt of Burlington, Vt.; and three grandchildren. "Frank McCourt, Whose Irish Childhood Illuminated His Prose, Is Dead at 78"

⟳ YOUR TURN

1. What change would correct the error in this sentence?

   > The old car needed new tires, furthermore, the paint was scratched, and the fender was bent.

   ○ A. Change the comma after *tires* to a semicolon.
   ○ B. Change the comma after *furthermore* to a semicolon.
   ○ C. Change the comma after *scratched* to a semicolon.
   ○ D. No change needs to be made to this sentence.

2. What change would correct the error in this sentence?

   > Jack has never been deliberately unkind; he is pleasant to everyone; friend or foe.

   ○ A. Change the semicolon after *unkind* to a comma.
   ○ B. Change both semicolons to commas.
   ○ C. Change the semicolon after *everyone* to a comma.
   ○ D. No change needs to be made to this sentence.

3. What change would correct the error in this sentence?

   > Janey's family moved into their new house along with Princess, their dog, Ginger, their cat; and Mason, their hamster.

   ○ A. Change the comma after *dog* to a semicolon.
   ○ B. Change the semicolon after *cat* to a comma.
   ○ C. Insert a semicolon after *house*.
   ○ D. No change needs to be made to this sentence.

4. What change would correct the error in this sentence?

   > Miguel's pirate costume was wonderful; he had even trained his pet parrot, Petey, to ride on his shoulder.

   ○ A. Change the semicolon after *wonderful* to a comma.
   ○ B. Change the commas around *Petey* to semicolons.
   ○ C. Insert a semicolon after *ride*.
   ○ D. No change needs to be made to this sentence.

Literary Analysis Writing Process: Edit and Publish

PLAN	DRAFT	REVISE	EDIT AND PUBLISH

You have revised your literary analysis essay based on your peer feedback and your own examination.

Now, it is time to edit your literary analysis essay. When you revised, you focused on the content of your literary analysis. You probably looked at your essay's claim, your organization, your supporting details and textual evidence, and your word choice. When you edit, you focus on the mechanics of your literary analysis essay, paying close attention to things like spelling, grammar, and punctuation. You can also edit to be sure your writing maintains a formal style and objective tone.

Use the checklist below to guide you as you edit:

☐ Have I spelled everything correctly?

☐ Have I correctly used capitalization throughout my essay?

☐ Have I used semicolons correctly to link closely related independent clauses and to create sentence variety?

☐ Have I used a consistent verb tense throughout the essay?

☐ Do I have any sentence fragments or run-on sentences?

☐ Have I maintained a formal style and objective tone?

Notice some edits Caroline has made:

- Replaced a pronoun to clarify a reference.

- Corrected her spelling after her spellchecker flagged some misspelled words.

- Checked and corrected her capitalization of words at the beginnings of sentences, following dashes, and in direct quotations.

- Correctly used a semicolon to correct a comma splice and show a connection between two complete thoughts.

- Changed a verb from past to present tense for consistency.

- Eliminated a contraction to maintain a formal style.

Please note that excerpts and passages in the StudySync® library and this workbook are intended as touchstones to generate interest in an author's work. The excerpts and passages do not substitute for the reading of entire texts, and StudySync® strongly recommends that students seek out and purchase the whole literary or informational work in order to experience it as the author intended. Links to online resellers are available in our digital library. In addition, complete works may be ordered through an authorized reseller by filling out and returning to StudySync® the order form enclosed in this workbook.

Reading & Writing Companion

137

Throughout his speech, ~~he~~ Henry uses the image of heavy chains to argue that the Americans are enslaved to ~~Britian~~ Britain. He asks, "~~is~~ Is life so dear, or peace so sweet, as to be purchased at the price of chains and slavery?" He declares that "if we wish to be free" then "we must fight!" ~~hH~~He ends his speech by speaking for himself: "I know not what course others may take; but as for me, give me liberty or give me death!" It is ~~like~~ as if he ~~didn't~~ does not care whether the others ~~folow~~ follow him~~;~~; he knows ~~what he will do. He has convinced himself to~~ that he will take ~~couragous~~ courageous action.

✏ WRITE

Use the questions on the previous page, as well as your peer reviews, to help you evaluate your literary analysis essay to determine areas that need editing. Then edit your literary analysis text to correct those errors.

Once you have made all your corrections, you are ready to publish your work. You can distribute your writing to family and friends, hang it on a bulletin board, or post it on your blog. If you publish online, share the link with your family, friends, and classmates.

Roosevelts on the Radio

INFORMATIONAL TEXT

Introduction

A week after his inauguration, President Franklin Delano Roosevelt gave his first "fireside chat" to the nation over the radio. He, along with First Lady Eleanor, began an unprecedented series of radio addresses delivered directly to the American people. Their influence changed how Americans expect their politicians to communicate.

V VOCABULARY

broadcasting
communicating to the public through radio or television

proficiency
expertise or skill

constituents
people who live and vote in an area

infamy
the state of being well-known for disgraceful character or actions

goodwill
a kind or helpful feeling

NOTES

☰ READ

1   Every Saturday morning from 2009 to 2016, Americans could turn on their radios and hear a weekly address from President Barack Obama. The practice of using the radio to reach Americans started in the 20th century. Franklin Delano Roosevelt was president from 1933 to 1945. He, along with his wife Eleanor, pioneered and perfected **broadcasting** from the Oval Office.

2   President Roosevelt and his wife Eleanor Roosevelt each made about 300 radio appearances during his 12 years in office. By 1940, most American homes had a radio. The radio was a great way for the president to reach people. It was inexpensive and efficient. He could speak directly to **constituents** without going through journalists.

3   Of all his radio appearances, President Roosevelt is most famous for his "fireside chats." These were a series of informal speeches to the nation. (The president did not sit next to a roaring fire during these chats. He sat at his desk behind microphones.) President Roosevelt needed to reassure a country reeling from the Great Depression. As a result, the tone of his chats was different than most

presidential speeches. He opened with the welcoming greeting "my friends." He did not use forceful language. Instead, he spoke calmly.

4   The chats were very successful. President Roosevelt was asked to speak every month or every week. He refused. He gave only a few chats a year. He wanted to make them special events. It worked. By some estimates, his most popular broadcasts reached 70 percent of radio listeners. He was a natural, confident speaker. The chats helped to increase public opinion of him.

5   Mrs. Roosevelt, on the other hand, was not a natural public speaker. Yet she became a popular radio personality too. Mrs. Roosevelt did 13 radio shows for women in 1932. After the success of those shows, she was regularly asked to do more. Mrs. Roosevelt talked about topics ranging from the challenges working women face to world peace. She rarely spoke directly about her husband's policies. Her popularity built **goodwill** for him.

6   Some people thought that Mrs. Roosevelt's radio shows were inappropriate for a First Lady. They were sponsored. She was paid for them. But not all of her radio appearances were for money. Both Roosevelts regularly appeared on air to host events and support charities.

7   The Roosevelts were very connected to the American people thanks to their radio **proficiency**. They got a lot of mail. President Roosevelt could receive 8,000 letters a day. Some previous administrations only received 200 letters in a week. Mrs. Roosevelt received 300,000 letters and postcards in 1933 alone. Many of the letters were negative. The Roosevelts were both hated and loved, like any politicians. But many letters were heartbreaking requests for help during hard times.

8   On December 7, 1941, the Japanese bombed the American naval base Pearl Harbor. Many Americans know the speech that President Roosevelt gave the next day. He called December 7 "a date which will live in **infamy**." The night of the attack, Mrs. Roosevelt addressed the nation. She had a regular Sunday night program. She spoke frankly to worried mothers and nervous young adults. She encouraged them to keep their spirits high. She said she was confident in the country.

9   President Roosevelt continued his "fireside chats" and radio broadcasts throughout World War II. When he died in 1945, most Americans grieved. They felt he had personally guided them through the challenges of the past decade.

10 Mrs. Roosevelt returned to the radio with a daily show in 1948. When television became more popular than radio, she appeared on television often. Polls ranked Mrs. Roosevelt as the most admired woman in the United States after her death in 1962. Thanks to radio, the Roosevelts had been welcomed into American homes. They left their mark.

First Read

Read the text. After you read, complete the Think Questions below.

☁ THINK QUESTIONS

1. Which two presidents are compared in the text?

   The text compares _____

   _____.

2. Write two or three sentences to describe the "fireside chats."

   The fireside chats were _____

   _____.

3. Why did Americans grieve when Roosevelt died in 1945? Support your answer with evidence from the text.

   Americans grieved because _____

   _____.

4. Use context to confirm the meaning of the word *proficiency* as it is used in "Roosevelts on the Radio." Write your definition of *proficiency* here.

   Proficiency means _____

   _____.

   A context clue is _____

   _____.

5. What is another way to say that fireside chats created *goodwill* toward the Roosevelts?

   Fireside chats _____

   _____.

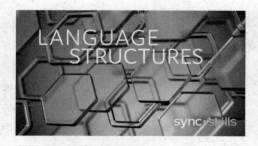

Skill:
Language Structures

★ DEFINE

In every language, there are rules that tell how to **structure** sentences. These rules define the correct order of words. In the English language, for example, a **basic** structure for sentences is subject, verb, and object. Some sentences have more **complicated** structures.

You will encounter both basic and complicated **language structures** in the classroom materials you read. Being familiar with language structures will help you better understand the text.

••• CHECKLIST FOR LANGUAGE STRUCTURES

To improve your comprehension of language structures, do the following:

✓ Monitor your understanding.

- Ask yourself: Why do I not understand this sentence? Is it because I do not understand some of the words? Or is it because I do not understand the way the words are ordered in the sentence?

✓ Break down the sentence into its parts.

- In English, many sentences share this basic pattern: subject + verb + object.

  > The **subject** names who or what is doing the action.

  > The **verb** names the action or state of being.

  > The **object** answers questions such as Who?, What?, Where?, and When?

- Ask yourself: What is the action? Who or what is doing the action? What details do the other words provide?

✓ Confirm your understanding with a peer or teacher.

Please note that excerpts and passages in the StudySync® library and this workbook are intended as touchstones to generate interest in an author's work. The excerpts and passages do not substitute for the reading of entire texts, and StudySync® strongly recommends that students seek out and purchase the whole literary or informational work in order to experience it as the author intended. Links to online resellers are available in our digital library. In addition, complete works may be ordered through an authorized reseller by filling out and returning to StudySync® the order form enclosed in this workbook.

Reading & Writing Companion   **143**

YOUR TURN

Read paragraph 8 from "Roosevelts on the Radio." Then, complete the chart by sorting the words and phrases into the "Subject," "Verb," and "Object" columns. The first row has been done as an example.

---

from "Roosevelts on the Radio"

On December 7, 1941, the Japanese bombed the American naval base Pearl Harbor. Many Americans know the speech that President Roosevelt gave the next day. He called December 7 "a date which will live in infamy." The night of the attack, Mrs. Roosevelt addressed the nation. She had a regular Sunday night program.

Options			
know	December 7 "a date which will live in infamy"	Many Americans	He
a regular Sunday night program	She	the speech	Mrs. Roosevelt
the nation	had	called	addressed

Sentence	Subject	Verb	Object
On December 7, 1941, the Japanese bombed the American naval base Pearl Harbor.	the Japanese	bombed	the American naval base Pearl Harbor
Many Americans know the speech that President Roosevelt gave the next day.			
He called December 7 "a date which will live in infamy."			
The night of the attack, Mrs. Roosevelt addressed the nation.			
She had a regular Sunday night program.			

Skill:
Conveying Ideas

★ DEFINE

Conveying ideas means communicating a **message** to another person. When speaking, you might not know what word to use to convey your ideas. When you do not know the exact English word, you can try different strategies. For example, you can ask for help from classmates or your teacher. You may use gestures and physical movements to act out the word. You can also try using **synonyms** or **defining** and describing the meaning you are trying to express.

••• CHECKLIST FOR CONVEYING IDEAS

To convey ideas for words you do not know when speaking, use the following learning strategies:

✓ Request help.

✓ Use gestures or physical movements.

✓ Use a synonym for the word.

✓ Describe what the word means using other words.

✓ Give an example of the word you want to use.

Please note that excerpts and passages in the StudySync® library and this workbook are intended as touchstones to generate interest in an author's work. The excerpts and passages do not substitute for the reading of entire texts, and StudySync® strongly recommends that students seek out and purchase the whole literary or informational work in order to experience it as the author intended. Links to online resellers are available in our digital library. In addition, complete works may be ordered through an authorized reseller by filling out and returning to StudySync® the order form enclosed in this workbook.

Reading & Writing
Companion

145

↻ YOUR TURN

Match each example with the correct strategy for conveying the meaning of the word *confident*.

A	The person uses the similar word *self-assured*.
B	The person mimes standing up straight and looking fearless.
C	The person explains that the word means "feeling sure of oneself."
D	The person says it is like when you have studied thoroughly and know you will do well on a test.

Strategies	Examples
Use gestures or physical movements.	
Use a synonym for the word.	
Describe what the word means using other words.	
Give an example of the word you want to use.	

Close Read

✏ WRITE

INFORMATIONAL: President Franklin Delano Roosevelt and his wife, Eleanor, used radio to communicate with the American people. In a short essay, explain why the "fireside chats" were successful. Use evidence from the text to convey your ideas. Pay attention to and edit for spelling patterns as you write.

Use the checklist below to guide you as you write:

☐ How did the Roosevelts use the radio?

☐ Who listened to the "fireside chats"?

☐ What made the chats popular?

Use the sentence frames to organize and write your informational text.

Many Americans had _____.

President Roosevelt's fireside chats were _____

_____.

President Roosevelt was a _____ speaker.

The tone of the broadcasts was _____.

The fireside chats improved _____ of him.

Please note that excerpts and passages in the StudySync® library and this workbook are intended as touchstones to generate interest in an author's work. The excerpts and passages do not substitute for the reading of entire texts, and StudySync® strongly recommends that students seek out and purchase the whole literary or informational work in order to experience it as the author intended. Links to online resellers are available in our digital library. In addition, complete works may be ordered through an authorized reseller by filling out and returning to StudySync® the order form enclosed in this workbook.

Reading & Writing Companion

147

The Dinner of the Lion

FICTION

Introduction

A lion demands honor and respect from animals who are destined to be his dinner. Will they bow before him and be eaten? Or will one of them come up with a solution to this big, furry problem?

V VOCABULARY

dread
a strong feeling of fear or worry

logic
a reasonable way of thinking

diminish
to decrease or reduce

measure
action taken as a way to achieve a goal

flattery
praise that is insincere

☰ READ

NOTES

1   The water was pure, and the grass was green. Life was marvelous for the animals in the Seven Hills, until the lion moved in. He believed he was the strongest and the most beautiful of all animals. His long, yellow mane rippled in the breeze like a flag announcing his greatness.

2   Lion believed he could do whatever he liked. He liked making others afraid. He insisted on being called "His Lordship." Even worse, he devoured two or three animals every day, creating great **dread** among them all. They became so frightened that they could hardly eat. The quality of the lion's meals **diminished**. His Lordship roared in fury, and the sound echoed in the hills like nearby thunder.

3   The fearful animals held a meeting. It would be easier to please the lion if only one animal were eaten a day. Then more might survive to see their children grow up. Weasel was sent to negotiate with His Lordship.

4   "Your honor," he began, "we fear for your health. The quality of your meals is poor. We suggest that, instead of you hunting down two or three of us, we will bring you one plump and extremely tender animal every day. You won't have to waste your time hunting. You are too great for such nonsense."

5   His Lordship, soaking up **flattery** like a sponge, agreed, adding a threat: "My meal must arrive on time. Bring it with the honor that is due me. I am great and deserve respect! If you disappoint me, I will eat all of you in a single day." Weasel retired from His Lordship's presence, bowing in obedience.

6   When Weasel reported back to the animals, they were torn between two feelings. It was better that only one of them got eaten every day. However, if His Lordship was not happy, they would all die. Only Hare saw the faulty **logic**.

7   "If he ate all of us," Hare explained, "there would be no more food. He would die too. He enjoys threatening others with extreme, but unlikely **measures**."

8   The animals still lived in fear of angering His Lordship. Each day they picked a name from a bowl to see who would be on the day's menu. Each one worried, thinking, "Tomorrow it may be my turn. I will never see my children again."

9   Everyone worried except Hare. When it was his turn, he seemed as tranquil as a summer breeze. He said, "I have a plan."

10   Hare dashed to the river and jumped in. Then he rolled around on the riverbank until his whole body except for his head was covered with smelly mud. Satisfied, Hare strolled toward His Lordship's den. He began to run when he got close. Appearing out of breath, he threw himself at His Lordship's feet.

11   "How dare you present me with a dirty meal!" His Lordship bellowed.

12   "Forgive me, oh great His Lordship who is the Greatest," Hare panted. "I am not the dinner. Another lion stole the delicious hare I was bringing you! He was bigger and stronger than you. His yellow mane blew so beautifully in the breeze."

13   His Lordship screamed in fury. "I am the GREATEST! No other lion is allowed in these hills! Show me that evil lion, and I will destroy him!"

14   Hare led the way to the old well. "He took your dinner and jumped in," Hare said, pretending to be frightened.

15　His Lordship looked into the well, and Hare peered over the edge at the same time. They saw the reflections of a lion and a neat, clean hare's head. "I will smash you because I am the Great Lion who owns these hills!" shrieked His Lordship. With that he hurled himself into the well and was never seen again.

16　The animals had a pleasant party that evening, and Hare lived to see his children, his grandchildren, and even his great grandchildren grow up.

Please note that excerpts and passages in the StudySync® library and this workbook are intended as touchstones to generate interest in an author's work. The excerpts and passages do not substitute for the reading of entire texts, and StudySync® strongly recommends that students seek out and purchase the whole literary or informational work in order to experience it as the author intended. Links to online resellers are available in our digital library. In addition, complete works may be ordered through an authorized reseller by filling out and returning to StudySync® the order form enclosed in this workbook.

Reading & Writing Companion　151

First Read

Read the story. After you read, complete the Think Questions below.

☁ THINK QUESTIONS

1. What was life like for the animals before Lion moved in?

   Life for the animals was _____

   _____.

2. Why are the animals scared of the lion?

   All the animals are afraid because _____

   _____.

3. How does Hare trick His Lordship?

   Hare tricks His Lordship by _____

   _____.

4. Use context to confirm the meaning of the word *logic* as it is used in "The Dinner of the Lion." Write your definition of *logic* here.

   Logic means _____

   _____.

   A context clue is _____

   _____.

5. What is another way to say that the rain *diminished*?

   The rain _____

   _____.

Skill: Analyzing Expressions

★ DEFINE

When you read, you may find English expressions that you do not know. An **expression** is a group of words that communicates an idea. Three types of expressions are idioms, sayings, and figurative language. They can be difficult to understand because the meanings of the words are different from their **literal**, or usual, meanings.

An **idiom** is an expression that is commonly known among a group of people. For example, "It's raining cats and dogs" means it is raining heavily. **Sayings** are short expressions that contain advice or wisdom. For instance, "Don't count your chickens before they hatch" means do not plan on something good happening before it happens. **Figurative** language is when you describe something by comparing it with something else, either directly (using the words *like* or *as*) or indirectly. For example, "I'm as hungry as a horse" means I'm very hungry. None of the expressions are about actual animals.

••• CHECKLIST FOR ANALYZING EXPRESSIONS

To determine the meaning of an expression, remember the following:

 If you find a confusing group of words, it may be an expression. The meaning of words in expressions may not be their literal meaning.

- Ask yourself: Is this confusing because the words are new? Or because the words do not make sense together?

✓ Determining the overall meaning may require that you use one or more of the following:

- context clues
- a dictionary or other resource
- teacher or peer support

✓ Highlight important information before and after the expression to look for clues.

Please note that excerpts and passages in the StudySync® library and this workbook are intended as touchstones to generate interest in an author's work. The excerpts and passages do not substitute for the reading of entire texts, and StudySync® strongly recommends that students seek out and purchase the whole literary or informational work in order to experience it as the author intended. Links to online resellers are available in our digital library. In addition, complete works may be ordered through an authorized reseller by filling out and returning to StudySync® the order form enclosed in this workbook.

Reading & Writing Companion   **153**

↻ YOUR TURN

Read paragraphs 5–9 from the story. Then, complete the multiple-choice questions below.

---

from **"The Dinner of the Lion"**

His Lordship, soaking up flattery like a sponge, agreed, adding a threat: "My meal must arrive on time. Bring it with the honor that is due me. I am great and deserve respect! If you disappoint me, I will eat all of you in a single day." Weasel retired from His Lordship's presence, bowing in obedience.

When Weasel reported back to the animals, they were torn between two feelings. It was better that only one of them got eaten every day. However, if His Lordship was not happy, they would all die. Only Hare saw the faulty logic.

"If he ate all of us," Hare explained, "there would be no more food. He would die too. He enjoys threatening others with extreme, but unlikely measures."

The animals still lived in fear of angering His Lordship. Each day they picked a name from a bowl to see who would be on the day's menu. Each one worried, thinking, "Tomorrow it may be my turn. I will never see my children again."

Everyone worried except Hare. When it was his turn, he seemed as tranquil as a summer breeze. He said, "I have a plan."

---

1. In paragraph 5, which sentence contains figurative language?

   ○ A. His Lordship, soaking up flattery like a sponge, agreed, adding a threat: "My meal must arrive on time."

   ○ B. "I am great and deserve respect!"

   ○ C. "If you disappoint me, I will eat all of you in a single day."

   ○ D. Weasel retired from His Lordship's presence, bowing in obedience.

2. Which word in paragraph 5 is a clue that one thing is being compared to another?

   ○ A. like

   ○ B. adding

   ○ C. due

   ○ D. single

3. If Hare seems "as tranquil as a summer breeze," how does he act?

○ A. cleverly

○ B. hotly

○ C. freely

○ D. calmly

4. Which figurative language best describes Lion?

○ A. as happy as a clam

○ B. as dry as a bone

○ C. as greedy as a pig

○ D. as busy as a bee

Skill:
Retelling and Summarizing

★ DEFINE

You can retell and summarize a text after reading to show your understanding. **Retelling** is telling a story again in your own words. **Summarizing** is giving a short explanation of the most important ideas in a text.

Keep your retelling or summary **concise**. Only include important information and key words from the text. By summarizing and retelling a text, you can improve your comprehension of the text's ideas.

••• CHECKLIST FOR RETELLING AND SUMMARIZING

In order to retell or summarize a text, note the following:

✓ Identify the main events of the text.

  • Ask yourself: What happens in this text? What are the main events that happen at the beginning, the middle, and the end of the text?

✓ Identify the main ideas in a text.

  • Ask yourself: What are the most important ideas in the text?

✓ Determine the answers to the six WH questions.

  • Ask yourself: After reading this text, can I answer Who?, What?, Where?, When?, Why?, and How? questions.

YOUR TURN

Read paragraphs 12–15 from the story. Then, complete the multiple-choice questions below.

---

from **"The Dinner of the Lion"**

"Forgive me, oh great His Lordship who is the Greatest," Hare panted. "I am not the dinner. Another lion stole the delicious hare I was bringing you! He was bigger and stronger than you. His yellow mane blew so beautifully in the breeze."

His Lordship screamed in fury. "I am the GREATEST! No other lion is allowed in these hills! Show me that evil lion, and I will destroy him!"

Hare led the way to the old well. "He took your dinner and jumped in," Hare said, pretending to be frightened.

His Lordship looked into the well, and Hare peered over the edge at the same time. They saw the reflections of a lion and a neat, clean hare's head. "I will smash you because I am the Great Lion who owns these hills!" shrieked His Lordship. With that he hurled himself into the well and was never seen again.

---

1. Who must be included in a summary of these paragraphs?

   ○ A. the two lions
   ○ B. Weasel and Hare
   ○ C. Hare and His Lordship
   ○ D. His Lordship and the imaginary lion

2. Which sentence best summarizes why His Lordship is angry?

   ○ A. He thinks that Hare has tricked him again.
   ○ B. He believes that another lion stole his dinner.
   ○ C. He knows that Hare is just pretending to be afraid.
   ○ D. He wants to eat Hare, but Hare is too small.

Please note that excerpts and passages in the StudySync® library and this workbook are intended as touchstones to generate interest in an author's work. The excerpts and passages do not substitute for the reading of entire texts, and StudySync® strongly recommends that students seek out and purchase the whole literary or informational work in order to experience it as the author intended. Links to online resellers are available in our digital library. In addition, complete works may be ordered through an authorized reseller by filling out and returning to StudySync® the order form enclosed in this workbook.

Reading & Writing Companion   **157**

3. Which statement is the main idea in these paragraphs?

   ○ A. Hare manages to trick His Lordship and save himself.
   ○ B. His Lordship is so greedy that he tries to eat another lion.
   ○ C. Hare uses His Lordship to get rid of the evil lion.
   ○ D. His Lordship proves that he is the greatest.

4. What is the best summary of these paragraphs?

   ○ A. When His Lordship wants food, he calls for Hare to bring it. Hare lies about the disappearance of the food, and instead of feeding him, he pushes the lion into a well.
   ○ B. His Lordship is about to eat Hare when the clever rabbit tells him about a fatter, juicier rabbit down in a well. The lion peers into the well and jumps in, never to be seen again.
   ○ C. Hare convinces His Lordship that he was not the meal the lion was supposed to eat. The lion becomes enraged and leaps into a well, never to be seen again.
   ○ D. To save himself from being eaten, Hare pretends that another lion stole His Lordship's meal. He leads the lion to a well. His Lordship sees his reflection and jumps in, never to be seen again.

Close Read

 WRITE

NARRATIVE: Retell the fable from the point of view of the Lion. How does he perceive the problem and the solutions? Use the characters, settings, and sequence of events from the original text. Pay attention to verb tenses as you write.

Use the checklist below to guide you as you write.

☐ Imagine that you are the lion. What problems do you face in Seven Hills?

☐ From Lion's point of view, what do you think about Weasel's solution?

☐ How do your feelings change as new events happen?

Use the sentence frames to organize and write your narrative.

When I first came to Seven Hills, I believed that I_____

_____.

When the animals got scared and stopped eating, I felt very _____

_____.

I was glad when Weasel _____. But when Hare arrived all muddy,

I felt _____. His story about the other lion made me feel

_____, because _____.

PHOTO/IMAGE CREDITS:

Cover, iStock.com/xijian
cover, ©iStock.com/eyewave, ©iStock.com/subjug,
©iStock.com/lvantsov, iStock.com/borchee, ©iStock.com/
seb_ra
p. iii, iStock.com/DNY59
p. iv, iStock.com/DWalker44
p. v, iStock.com/DWalker44
p. v, iStock.com/deimagine
p. vi, iStock.com/DWalker44
p. vi, ©iStock.com/halbergman
p. vi, iStock.com/DragonImages
p. vi, iStock.com/Petar Chernaev
p. vi, iStock.com/Kirby Hamilton
p. vi, iStock.com/EricFerguson
p. vii, iStock.com/hanibaram, iStock.com/seb_ra, iStock.
com/Martin Barraud
p. ix, iStock.com/xijian
p. x, Chinua Achebe - Eliot Elisofon/Contributor/The LIFE
Picture Collection/Getty Images
p. x, Hayan Charara - Rachel de Cordova
p. x, Joseph Conrad - George C. Beresford/Stringer/
Hulton Archive/Getty Images
p. x, Patrick Henry - benoitb/DigitalVision Vectors/Getty
Images
p. x, Franz Kafka - Stringer/Contributor/Hulton Archive/
Getty Archive Photos/
p. xi, Mohja Kahf - courtesy of Wendi La Fey
p. xi, Martin Luther King Jr. - Bettmann/Contributor/
Bettmann/Getty Images
p. xi, Francis La Flesche - Public Domain
p. xi, Ursula K. LeGuin - Michael Buckner/Stringer/Getty
Images North America
p. 0, ©iStock.com/DWalker44
p. 5, ©iStock.com/Delpixart/
p. 6, ©iStock.com/Delpixart/
p. 7, ©iStock.com/DWalker44
p. 8, ©istock.com/urbancow
p. 9, ©istock.com/urbancow
p. 10, ©iStock.com/deimagine
p. 11, ©iStock.com/deimagine
p. 12, ©iStock.com/DWalker44
p. 13, ©istock.com/diegograndi
p. 15, Getty: NurPhoto/Contributor/NurPhoto
p. 16, Getty: AFP/Stringer/AFP
p. 18, ©istock.com/diegograndi
p. 19, ©istock.com/PetarPaunchev
p. 22, ©istock.com/RapidEye
p. 26, ©istock.com/RapidEye
p. 27, ©istock.com/ooyoo
p. 28, ©istock.com/ooyoo
p. 29, ©iStock.com/Dominique_Lavoie
p. 30, ©iStock.com/Dominique_Lavoie
p. 31, ©iStock.com/Martin Barraud
p. 32, ©iStock.com/Martin Barraud
p. 34, ©iStock.com/RapidEye
p. 35, ©istock.com/MidwestWilderness
p. 36, Public Domain
p. 41, ©istock.com/funky-data
p. 45, ©istock.com/
p. 48, ©istock.com/Rauluminate
p. 49, ©iStock.com/Dominique_Lavoie

p. 50, ©iStock.com/Dominique_Lavoie
p. 51, ©iStock.com/yipengge
p. 52, ©iStock.com/yipengge
p. 53, ©istock.com/
p. 54, ©iStock.com/jdemast
p. 58, ©iStock.com/dblight
p. 63, Bettmann/Contributor/Getty Images
p. 78, Bettmann/Contributor/Getty Images
p. 79, ©iStock.com/ThomasVogel
p. 80, ©iStock.com/ThomasVogel
p. 81, ©iStock.com/DNY59
p. 82, ©iStock.com/DNY59
p. 83, ©iStock/pixhook
p. 84, ©iStock/pixhook
p. 85, Bettmann/Contributor/Getty Images
p. 86, ©iStock.com/GoodLifeStudio
p. 89, iStock.com/
p. 90, Public Domain
p. 93, iStock.com/
p. 94, ©iStock.com/Brostock
p. 95, ©iStock.com/Brostock
p. 96, ©iStock.com/antoni_halim
p. 97, ©iStock.com/antoni_halim
p. 98, ©iStock.com/Martin Barraud
p. 99, ©iStock.com/Martin Barraud
p. 100, ©iStock.com/
p. 102, ©iStock.com/hanibaram, iStock.com/seb_ra, iStock.
com/Martin Barraud
p. 103, ©iStock.com/Martin Barraud
p. 108, ©iStock.com/fstop123
p. 111, ©iStock.com/gopixa
p. 113, ©iStock.com/Dominik Pabis
p. 115, ©iStock.com/Martin Barraud
p. 119, ©iStock/bo1982
p. 121, ©iStock/Jeff_Hu
p. 124, ©iStock.com/stevedangers
p. 126, ©iStock.com/Martin Barraud
p. 128, iStock/Fodor90
p. 131, iStock.com/efks
p. 133, istock.com/
p. 135, iStock.com/Piotr_roae
p. 137, ©iStock.com/Martin Barraud
p. 139, ©iStock.com/halbergman
p. 140, iStock.com/
p. 140, iStock.com/
p. 140, iStock.com/
p. 140, iStock.com/
p. 140, iStock.com/
p. 142, ©iStock.com/halbergman
p. 143, ©iStock.com/BlackJack3D
p. 145, ©iStock.com/BlackJack3D
p. 147, ©iStock.com/halbergman
p. 148, ©iStock.com/EcoPic
p. 149, iStock.com/
p. 149, iStock.com/
p. 149, iStock.com/
p. 149, iStock.com/
p. 149, iStock.com/
p. 152, ©iStock.com/EcoPic
p. 153, ©iStock.com/Ales_Utovko
p. 156, ©iStock.com/eugenesergeev
p. 159, ©iStock.com/EcoPic

Text Fulfillment
Through StudySync

If you are interested in specific titles, please fill out the form below and we will check availability through our partners.

ORDER DETAILS

Date:

TITLE	AUTHOR	Paperback/ Hardcover	Specific Edition *If Applicable*	Quantity

SHIPPING INFORMATION

Contact:

Title:

School/District:

Address Line 1:

Address Line 2:

Zip or Postal Code:

Phone:

Mobile:

Email:

BILLING INFORMATION   ☐ *SAME AS SHIPPING*

Contact:

Title:

School/District:

Address Line 1:

Address Line 2:

Zip or Postal Code:

Phone:

Mobile:

Email:

PAYMENT INFORMATION

☐ CREDIT CARD

Name on Card:

Card Number: Expiration Date: Security Code:

☐ PO

Purchase Order Number:

StudySync Text Fulfillment, BookheadEd Learning, LLC
610 Daniel Young Drive | Sonoma, CA 95476